Advance Praise for *Step Into Leadership Greatness Volume 3,*
Be A Force Multiplier, Elevating Others to New Heights

Step Into Leadership Greatness Volume 3, Be a Force Multiplier, Elevating Others to New Heights is an inspiring and practical guide for leaders who want to empower their teams. This book is a must-read for anyone looking to step into leadership greatness and elevate others to their full potential.

Nurbanu Somani
London Organization of Skills Development

Must Read for Aspiring Professionals. "DJ" Jaeger shares a relatable and compelling story about the value of mentorship, presented with an easy and engaging flow. Her message will resonate strongly with ambitious professionals, highlighting the often-overlooked importance of seeking guidance and taking ownership of their career development."

Dr. Candace Steele Flippin
Founder, Global Career Advancement Institute

"Dr. Benjamin clearly explains the differences between mentoring, sponsorship, and coaching and, when used together, the power they have to elevate leaders, transform careers, and bring big dreams to life."

Audrey Coulbourn

"The Leadership Puzzle is a masterful exploration of guiding teams through empathy and connection, providing easy-to-implement frameworks for those seeking to inspire and influence others. Drawing on real-world experiences, the book illustrates how to align individual strengths with organizational goals. This impactful read is an essential resource for anyone looking to cultivate cohesive, resilient teams where every piece matters."

Tia Chaeng

Praise for Dr. Michelle Boulden-Hammond's Chapter, The Journey to Greatness: A Story of Elevation

Dr. Michelle Boulden-Hammond's chapter in Step Into Leadership Greatness, Be a Force Multiplier: Elevate Others to New Heights by Dr.

Jennifer Jones Bryant is nothing short of inspiring, spirit-lifting, and powerfully motivating. From the first paragraph, I felt as though she was personally coaching me toward the finish line of my next goal.

Her ability to break down complex concepts into bite-sized, practical steps makes the journey toward personal and professional greatness feel attainable and empowering. The chapter is filled with realistic, actionable strategies that help you recognize and cast down limiting beliefs. Dr. Michelle masterfully illustrates this with real-life scenarios that resonate deeply—reminding us all of challenges we've faced and offering solutions we can implement right now.

This chapter is a shining example of how to elevate oneself into becoming a true force multiplier. It is a must-read for anyone ready to step into their greatness and inspire others to do the same.

Dr. Alonda J. Ross-Brooks
WomenCeosROCK

Dr. Jennifer Bryant's book, Step Into Leadership Greatness, Be A Force Mulitplier, Elevate Others to New Heights, Mary Cary writes her chapter: Criticism to Confidence: A Journey to Leadership is a powerful exploration of the transformative impact of leadership rooted in intentionality and resilience. Drawing from deep personal experiences, Mary Cary shares how even the most challenging moments of leadership can ignite self-awareness, growth, and the desire to inspire others. Her concept of "force multiplier" leadership emphasizes building trust, fostering collaboration, and empowering individuals to thrive. This is done all while embracing the importance of vulnerability and authenticity. This book is an invaluable guide for leaders seeking to cultivate confidence, motivate teams, and create a legacy of empowerment. The wisdom will inspire readers to lead with courage, compassion, and clarity.

Dr. Stephanie M. Kirkland
Identity Dynamics®

Step Into Leadership Greatness

Be A Force Multiplier: Elevating Others to New Heights

Visionary Dr. Jennifer Jones Bryant

Foreword by Dr. Karen Hills Pruden

Step Into Leadership Greatness™ Be A Force Multiplier: Elevating Others to New Heights

©2025 by Dr. Jennifer Jones Bryant

All rights reserved. Printed in the United States of America

No part of this publication may be reproduced, distributed, or transmitted in any form or by any means, including photocopying, recording, or other electronic or mechanical methods, without the prior written permission of the publisher, except in cases of brief quotation embodied in the critical reviews and specific noncommercial uses permitted by copyright law.

ISBN: 979-830-823-9482

Table of Contents

A Special Message to the Readers — 3

A Step Into Leadership Greatness Poem — 4

Dedication — 5

Special Dedication — 7

Foreword — 8

Dr. Karen Hills Pruden

Introduction — 12

Dr. Jennifer Jones Bryant

Transformational Leadership and Empowerment

- Dr. Theresa A. Moseley — 21
- The Honorable Savannah Winston — 27
- Dr. Rhonda M. Wood — 34
- Naomi Carrington-Hockman — 41

The Leadership Trifecta (Mentorship, Sponsorship, and Coaching)

- Dr. Tilantine Benjamin — 50
- Danielle "DJ" Jaeger — 57
- Dr. Michelle Boulden Hammond — 63
- Tamera P. Jones — 69

Vision, Mindset, and Growth

- Dr. Adebola Ajao — 78

Mary E. Cary	85
Dr. Nadia Monsano	91
Katrina Tasby	97
LuDrean Howard Peterson	101
Reflection Page with Questions	**109**

A Special Message to Our Readers

Thank you for picking up *Step Into Leadership Greatness, Be a Force Multiplier: Elevating Others to New Heights, Volume 3* series. By doing so, you are not only investing in your own growth and leadership journey but also helping to empower others in meaningful ways.

A portion of the proceeds from this book will be donated to the *Step Into Leadership Greatness Foundation Inc.*™, a 501(C) (3) nonprofit. The foundation is committed to providing resources, mentorship, and support to leaders seeking to develop their leadership skills. Your purchase will directly contribute to fostering the next generation of leaders, helping them unlock their full potential, and creating a ripple effect of positive change.

With your support, we can continue to nurture leaders who will uplift, inspire, and serve their communities with purpose and passion. Thank you for participating in this movement and investing in a brighter, more empowered future for all.

Together, we are stepping into greatness—one leader at a time.

With heartfelt gratitude,

Dr. Jennifer Jones Bryant

Founder, *Step Into Leadership Greatness Foundation Inc.*

We gladly welcome your generosity; every gift makes a difference: https://www.stepintoleadershipfoundation.org/donate

Step into Leadership Greatness Poem

Step into Leadership Greatness, with courage and grace,
A leader's path is not one to chase.
It's built with vision, strong and clear,
A beacon for others, drawing them near.

Stand tall in the face of doubt and fear,
For growth is born when we persevere.
Each challenge a lesson, each setback a guide,
With every misstep, let wisdom reside.

Lead with purpose, ignite the spark,
In others, it is a fire that leaves its mark.
Lift them higher, show them the way,
Guide them through night, into the day.

Listen with empathy, speak with truth,
Encourage the dreamers ignite their youth.
Make space for voices, let them be heard,
In the chorus of leaders, find your word.

In service to others, the journey unfolds,
With every decision, a story is told.
Be the force that inspires and grows,
For greatness is found where kindness flows.

Step into Leadership Greatness, don't wait for the sign,
Lead with your heart, and the stars will align.
In the hands of a leader, the world comes to bloom—
Step forth in your power and watch the light loom.

Dr. Jennifer Jones Bryant

Dedication

This book, and all the work that flows from it, is dedicated to the incredible forces that have shaped my journey—each of you has inspired, empowered, and supported me in ways words can scarcely capture.

To my late mother, Queen Esther Baxter, you were the heart of my strength. Your perseverance and determination instilled in me a deep belief in pushing forward, no matter the obstacles. It is because of you that I found the courage to launch the *Step Into Leadership Greatness Foundation Inc.*, carrying with me the wisdom and lessons you imparted. You are the spark that ignited this journey, and your legacy lives on in everything I do.

To my amazing husband, Anthony Gunter, your unwavering love, support, and belief in me have been the foundation of every step I've taken on this path. You are my rock, my greatest ally, and a constant source of inspiration. Thank you for walking beside me, lifting me when I faltered, and sharing in every triumph along the way. Your presence is a gift I treasure beyond measure.

To my beautiful daughters, Jayla and Harmony Bryant, you are my greatest purpose and my greatest joy. Your boundless energy, curiosity, and joy remind me every day of why I lead—with heart, passion, and vision. Watching you grow into strong, compassionate, and courageous leaders of tomorrow fills me with pride and hope. You are my legacy, and I know you will continue to inspire and change the world.

To the extraordinary authors of Step Into Leadership Greatness, together, we have created something truly special. Each of you has shared your wisdom, your stories, and your hearts, building a collective work that will inspire and elevate others for generations to come. Your courage to step into your own greatness empowered me to do the same, and for that, I am forever grateful.

And to the mentors, coaches, and sponsors who have invested in my leadership journey—Your belief in me has been a guiding light. You have equipped me to be a beacon of hope and inspiration for others. Your support has enabled me to motivate, empower, and encourage those I lead to reach higher, rise stronger, and dream bigger. Thank you for your guidance, generosity, and willingness to pour into me, so I, in turn, can pour into others.

This work—this mission—is a reflection of all of you. Together, we are creating a ripple effect as "*force multipliers*," leaving a legacy of leadership, service, and impact that will endure long after the pages are turned.

With deep love and immense gratitude,

Dr. Jennifer Jones Bryant

Special Dedication

Remembering Executive Pastor Dr. Davetta Henderson

Executive Pastor Dr. Davetta Henderson was a woman of unwavering grace, a sweet, gentle, and incredibly supportive soul who touched the lives of so many. Dr. Davetta truly stepped into her leadership greatness as a bestselling author and speaker with the *"Step Into Leadership Greatness"* community. Her words, wisdom, and passion for uplifting others will forever echo in the hearts of those she inspired. Her legacy lives on through the powerful impact of her work, which guides, encourages, and empowers others to step boldly into their own greatness.

Step on, Dr. Davetta. You have fought the good fight, finished the race, and kept the faith. Rest well, God's good and faithful servant.

Foreword
Dr. Karen Hills Pruden

Leadership is both an art and a science, an intentional journey filled with learning, unlearning, and growth. As leaders, we often find ourselves standing at the intersection of personal triumph and collective elevation, where our own experiences shape the foundation upon which others rise. It is in this space that the third volume of *Step Into Leadership Greatness* (SILG) emerges as a transformative guide for leaders who aspire to be force multipliers—those who elevate others to new heights.

Having had the honor of contributing to volumes one and two of Dr. Jennifer Jones Bryant's SILG series, I have witnessed firsthand the evolution of this profound body of work. In volume one, authors explored the essential truth that Leadership Isn't Just a Title, offering a foundation for understanding leadership as action and service. Volume two expanded this concept as we shared our insights on how Leaders Produce Leaders, emphasizing the cyclical nature of leadership that empowers others to lead. Now, with volume three, we arrive at a full-circle moment with the powerful theme of Be A Force Multiplier: Elevating Others to New Heights.

Volume 3 is a masterful tapestry of stories, strategies, and principles, woven together by leaders who have faced storms, embraced reflection, and emerged with clarity and purpose. Throughout these pages, you'll uncover recurring themes resonating with impactful leadership.

Reflection and Self-Discovery

Several authors highlight the importance of reflection and self-discovery as the cornerstones of personal and professional growth. They recount how navigating obstacles developed their resilience and self-awareness. One author poignantly notes that life's challenges provide essential lessons for self-development.

Mentorship and the Leadership Trifecta

Mentorship is a vital thread throughout the book. From parents and teachers modeling self-development to professional mentors navigating leadership's complexities, mentorship's impact is undeniable. One author introduces the 'Leadership Trifecta': problem-solving, guidance, and direction converging to create a transformative coaching experience.

Vision and Mindset

The chapters repeatedly emphasize the necessity of vision and mindset for leadership. As one author eloquently states, 'Clarity of vision must precede action.' This clarity guides purposeful leadership, aligning actions with values and goals.

Influence, Impact, and Purposeful Leadership

Influence and impact resonate throughout the book, reinforcing that leadership empowers others to unlock their potential. One author reminds us that 'leadership is a calling and a choice,' urging intentional purpose. Purpose, vision, and culture are intricately connected, creating the environment for shared growth and leadership development.

Criticism and Growth

The power of criticism is also explored as a tool for growth. One author shares how constructive criticism from a challenging boss elevated her confidence and competence, while another recounts how overcoming a toxic corporate culture propelled her into entrepreneurship, activating her force multiplier abilities.

Ultimately, Volume 3 underscores a profound truth: leadership is relational. Our connections and the environments we shape determine our influence and legacy. Through shared vision, transformational leadership, or developing others, this book challenges us to inspire and elevate those around us.

As you immerse yourself in the wisdom within these pages, consider how you, too, can be a force multiplier. Leadership is not a solitary endeavor, but a collective pursuit of greatness transcending individuals and elevating communities.

Relevance to the Book's Theme

The experiences in Volume 3 align directly with the theme of being a force multiplier. Through personal reflections, the authors demonstrate how self-awareness and resilience are foundational to leading others effectively. The emphasis on mentorship highlights its power to transform and develop future leaders, multiplying impact. Discussions on vision and mindset underscore the importance of strategic thinking and clarity for guiding teams toward shared goals. The exploration of influence and purposeful leadership shows how empowering others and fostering a positive environment leads to collective success. Moreover, narratives on criticism and growth reveal that challenges and feedback, integral to personal development, enable leaders to refine their approaches and better support their teams. This aligns with the concept of a force multiplier: enhancing others' capabilities leads to exponential improvements.

In essence, Dr. Bryant's Volume 3 comprehensively guides leaders seeking to elevate others through practical insights, personal experiences, and actionable strategies embodying effective and impactful leadership principles. Volume 3 perfectly complements the *Step Into Leadership Greatness* series, its theme anchoring the exploration of leadership's title and the recognition that extraordinary leaders produce leaders.

Dr. Karen Hills Pruden

Dr. Karen Hills Pruden is the CEO of Pruden Global Business Solutions Consulting DBA Sister Leaders, a leadership training and professional development organization, committed to strategizing with high-performing professionals to elevate their careers or business. Imagine being stuck and feeling the weight of being underutilized by your employer. That's where Dr. Karen steps in. She's on a mission to help high-performing leaders maximize using their professional knowledge and experience to create and leverage their professional identity and reputation. She accomplishes this by sharing her Amplify Your Value 5-Step Framework.

Dr. Karen has worked in leadership in the tax industry, retail industry, non-profit, museums, and higher education. Dr. Karen has authored/co-authored 30+ books, most of which are bestsellers. Her latest publication in her Amplify Your Value Series, The Comprehensive Business Audit Checklist, was published in October 2024.

Websites: https://www.drkarenhillspruden.com

Introduction

Step Into Leadership Greatness – Be A Force Multiplier

Dr. Jennifer Jones Bryant

Leadership is not merely a position or a title—it's a responsibility, a calling, and, most importantly, an opportunity to make an impact that inspires, empowers, and elevates those around you, creating a ripple effect that reaches far beyond your immediate influence. Leadership is also about human connection—seeing others as people first, understanding their unique needs and aspirations, and guiding them with empathy, respect, and understanding.

This anthology, *Step Into Leadership Greatness: Be A Force Multiplier to Elevate Others to New Heights*, is the third book in my Step Into Leadership Greatness series. It serves as a testament to the transformative power of leadership that focuses on personal success and elevates others. It creates a ripple effect, transcending your direct influence and leaving a lasting impact. Authentic leadership humanizes the process, recognizing that the greatest strength lies in empowering others to reach their full potential, not by commanding them but by truly understanding them.

At its core, being a force multiplier means amplifying the abilities, talents, and potential of others. It's about recognizing the greatness in people—even when they can't see it themselves—and helping them rise to their highest potential. Exceptional leaders set themselves apart by elevating others through mentorship, encouragement, or leading by example. When we lead with empathy, compassion, and humanity, we unlock the full power of our teams and ourselves.

This anthology brings together a diverse group of leaders who embody the principle of being a force multiplier. Each contributor shares their unique journey, insights, and strategies for fostering growth in others. From navigating challenges to celebrating triumphs, these stories highlight the meaning of leading with purpose, compassion, and intentionality. They reflect the human element of leadership—how each leader strives to make a positive impact on the lives of others.

The Formula for Being a Force Multiplier

Being a force multiplier as a leader is about combining the right elements to elevate yourself and everyone around you. This formula for leadership success can be expressed as:

Force Multiplier = (Clarity × Empowerment × Collaboration × Vision)

Here's a breakdown of each component:

1. **Clarity**
    - Define and communicate clear goals, priorities, and expectations.
    - Ensure your team understands the "why" behind their work.

2. **Empowerment**
    - Equip others with the tools, resources, and autonomy to succeed.
    - Foster a growth mindset and encourage continuous development.
    - Delegate strategically, trusting others to own their responsibilities.

3. **Collaboration**
    - Build and nurture a culture of teamwork.
    - Encourage the sharing of ideas and leveraging individual strengths for collective success.
    - Foster connections across networks to amplify impact.

4. **Vision**
    - Inspire others with a compelling vision of the future.
    - Align team efforts with this vision, creating a shared sense of purpose.
    - Demonstrate resilience and adaptability to navigate challenges while staying focused on the bigger picture.

When leaders combine these elements, they multiply their influence and the impact of their teams, enabling everyone to achieve greater results than they could individually. Authentic leadership goes beyond technical expertise and performance—it is about creating an environment where each person feels seen, valued, and supported in their growth.

The S.T.E.P. Framework: A Blueprint for Leadership Greatness

Central to this anthology is the **S.T.E.P. Framework**, a powerful model for stepping into leadership greatness:

- **S—Self-Awareness:** True leadership begins with knowing yourself—your strengths, your blind spots, and your unique leadership style. Self-awareness lays the foundation for authentic leadership and builds trust with others. It requires a deep understanding of one's humanity and the humility to lead from a place of empathy and authenticity.

- **T – Trust:** Great leaders cultivate trust, not only in themselves but also among their teams. Trust is the cornerstone of collaboration, communication, and mutual respect. Without trust, no amount of strategy or vision can move a team forward. Trust grows when leaders connect with people as individuals, not just as employees or followers.

- **E—Empowerment:** Leadership is more than overseeing tasks; it's about empowering others to reach their potential. When you empower others, you create an environment where everyone thrives. Empowerment means giving people the freedom to innovate, fail, and grow. It's about trusting others enough to help them realize their potential and step into their own leadership.

- **P – Purpose:** Purpose-driven leadership inspires others to achieve beyond their limits. When you lead with clarity, passion, and a focus on impact, you ignite purpose in those around you. Humanizing leadership means leading with heart—creating a vision that taps into the deeper motivations of individuals and fosters a sense of shared purpose that drives collective success.

The **S.T.E.P. Framework** is a holistic approach that transforms leadership from a personal endeavor into a shared journey of growth and success. It encourages leaders to take a human-centered approach that builds relationships, fosters growth and allows people to thrive as individuals and as part of a greater mission. Leadership greatness is not an isolated achievement but a collective one driven by authentic connections between people.

Introducing the Step Into Leadership Greatness Foundation, Inc.

This book marks the beginning of something even greater: The Step Into Leadership Greatness Foundation, Inc. The foundation was established with a clear mission: empowering emerging leaders, fostering mentorship, and creating a lasting impact through educational and leadership development programs.

At the heart of the foundation is the belief that leadership can be taught, cultivated, and expanded. The SILG Foundation aims to create a space where aspiring leaders—whether in business, education, non-profit work, or community organizations—can gain the tools, mentorship, and resources needed to amplify their influence as leaders and force multipliers. The foundation's work will focus on developing skills and competencies and fostering the emotional intelligence, self-awareness, and compassion that are key to humanizing leadership in today's world.

Through the foundation, we will provide:

- **Leadership Training and Development:** Workshops, seminars, and online courses designed to help individuals cultivate the core leadership principles outlined in this book and the S.T.E.P. Framework.

- **Mentorship Programs:** A platform to connect emerging leaders with experienced mentors who can guide them on their leadership journey.

- **Community Building:** Establishing a network of like-minded individuals committed to stepping into their leadership greatness, where they can collaborate, learn, and grow together.

- **Scholarships and Grants:** Offering financial assistance to individuals who need support in furthering their leadership education or entrepreneurial endeavors.

The **SILG Foundation Inc.** is committed to making leadership development accessible to all, especially those who might otherwise not have the resources or opportunities to cultivate their leadership skills. By doing so, we can expand the pool of force multipliers who will lead with purpose, and humanity, and impact their communities for years to come.

Conclusion: A Movement for Leadership Greatness

Leadership greatness is not achieved in isolation—it is cultivated through connection, collaboration, and the courage to lift others as we climb. By embracing the mindset of a force multiplier and applying the **S.T.E.P. Framework**, you'll elevate others to new heights and unlock new dimensions of your potential.

As you read through this anthology, you'll find the **S.T.E.P. Framework** woven throughout the stories and lessons shared by our contributors. Each narrative demonstrates how these principles can be applied in real-life scenarios, providing a blueprint for leadership greatness.

The **Step Into Leadership Greatness Foundation Inc.** will further support your journey by providing tools, resources, and a community of leaders dedicated to lifting others. Together, we can redefine leadership, inspire transformation, and create a lasting legacy of greatness that places people, connection, and purpose at the heart of everything we do.

Welcome to the movement. It's time to step into your leadership greatness.

Dr. Jennifer Jones Bryant

Dr. Jennifer Jones Bryant is a dynamic thought leader in empowerment and leadership coaching. As the Founder and President of the Step Into Leadership Greatness Foundation Inc., Dr. Bryant honors her late mother's legacy by providing scholarships to first-generation college students pursuing degrees in business management and leadership. Her foundation empowers future leaders to overcome barriers, achieve their dreams, and create a lasting impact.

Dr. Bryant is also the Executive Founder of Reaching Within, An Empowerment Journey LLC, where she helps individuals unlock their full potential and find personal and professional fulfillment. A 13X international best-selling author, Dr. Bryant has written transformative books that inspire and guide readers on their journey to self-discovery and growth. Her work has earned her multiple global awards and recognition as an ACC-certified life and leadership coach.

Dr. Bryant's corporate impact is equally impressive. As a senior leader with a Fortune 100 company, she drove initiatives to improve associate engagement, organizational culture, diversity, inclusion, and belonging. Her leadership extended to overseeing one of the largest women's empowerment business resource groups, uniting over 24,000 members globally.

Before transitioning to the private sector, Dr. Bryant built a distinguished 31-year career in the federal government, rising from clerk-typist to Executive Director. She consistently delivered exceptional results in business management, process improvements, and employee engagement within technology-driven organizations. Her accomplishments have been celebrated through numerous awards, including the Presidential Lifetime Achievement Award for her leadership, innovation, and contributions to civil rights and diversity initiatives.

Dr. Bryant holds a Master of Science in International Affairs, an executive leadership certification from American University, a Women in Entrepreneurship and Diversity, Inclusion and Belonging Certificate from Cornell University, and Doctorates in Leadership and Philosophy. She is a proud member of Zeta Phi Beta Sorority Inc.

A sought-after speaker and seasoned leader, Dr. Bryant frequently shares her expertise at federal agencies, universities, and community organizations. She has been featured in publications such as *Essence Magazine*, *Brainz Magazine*, and *VIP Global Magazine* and has appeared on platforms like Radio One, WTOP, and WUSA's Great Day Washington.

Dr. Bryant's work exemplifies a commitment to lifting others, building resilient leaders, and honoring her late mother's values of perseverance, love, and empowerment.

Contact: Dr. Jennifer Jones Bryant, Founder and President, SILG

SILG FB Page:
https://www.facebook.com/share/1LFfXogiZs/?mibextid=LQQJ4d

Website: https://www.stepintoleadershipfoundation.org/

Website: www.ReachingWithinEmpowerment.com

Linkedin: https://www.linkedin.com/in/dr-jenniferjonesbryant-15a7a622

Dr. Jennifer Jones Bryant FB page:
https://www.facebook.com/share/1WAQBcaui2/?mibextid=LQQJ4d

Transformational Leadership and Empowerment

The Art of Elevating Others Through Transformational Leadership

Dr. Theresa A. Moseley

"Transformational Leadership occurs where leaders focus on empowering people, not just what they can gain from their position." (Dr. Gift Gugu Mona, *The Effective Leadership Prototype for a Modern Day Leader* 2020) Dr. Mona describes leaders as thermostats that change to suit different situations. Adaptability is another way to describe her statement. As a transformational leader, she understands the importance of developing and empowering leaders in an organization to elevate others. Developing leaders is an art because it involves interpersonal dynamics and understanding human behavior, requiring the ability to navigate complex situations and understand the importance of emotional intelligence.

To grow its leaders, an organization must empower, encourage, develop the skills of, and support all employees. Elevating others is crucial because it fosters ownership and responsibility, builds a skilled workforce, cultivates valued relationships, and prepares future leaders for success through empowerment and mentorship.

Immediately after high school, I entered the military and was placed in a leadership role on my first day of basic training, where I discovered my innate leadership skills. I took the lead in organizing 40 wardrobes for our company, assigning roles based on strengths I identified by simply asking! From day one, I understood the importance of communication and collaboration. Military service reinforced the importance of communication, active listening, adaptability, and collaboration for developing future leaders.

As a high school principal, I focused on building the capacity of my administrative team. Our weekly professional development emphasized communication, collaboration, and creativity, aligning with the tenets of Transformational Leadership: Individual Consideration (fostering open communication and support), Intellectual Stimulation (encouraging creative problem-solving), and Inspirational Motivation (articulating a shared vision and motivating collaborative goal achievement). During my 27-year career in education, I trained numerous administrators, vice principals, and graduate students on the tenets of Transformational Leadership, encouraging them to utilize these best practices to elevate others.

Developing team members and helping them reach their potential is incredibly rewarding. Effective leaders understand how to achieve this success, benefiting both the organization and its aspiring leaders. As principal, our administrative team enhanced existing systems like collaborative planning and team meetings to address the school's needs. We implemented monthly professional development informed by learning walks and individual teacher meetings, triangulating data to improve student achievement. Weekly meetings with assistant principals focused on developing their leadership skills and empowering them to provide effective feedback to teachers.

A rewarding experience involved mentoring a first-year assistant principal on providing effective feedback. After our training, a teacher praised his thoroughness, action steps, and curriculum knowledge during a post-observation conference. This demonstrated the direct impact of the training, ensuring he will continue to train and empower others as he advances.

In schools, there are always problems to solve, whether academic or related to climate and culture. We always used creativity to problem-solve. One of my concerns during my first year as principal was the number of repeat offenders from the previous year. I questioned why there were so many. One reason given was a lack of follow-up after students returned from suspension. As a result, we implemented a quarterly ROSE Day (Repeat Offender Support Effort). During this meeting, parents were invited with the student, teacher, guidance counselor, and administrator to discuss the concern. We discussed the root cause of the incidents that led to suspensions, attendance, grades, motivation, and individual goals for the students. ROSE Day was an excellent example of collaboration and creativity, allowing all stakeholders to address their concerns. As the school leader, I modeled ways to improve communication and problem-solving through collaboration.

To elevate your team members and empower others to achieve success, I recommend the following tips and strategies:

1. **Establish Trust:** Always be authentic. Get to know your employees and understand their strengths and areas for growth. Be benevolent, reliable, open, and honest. Always do what you say you will do. Surround yourself with people you trust and who are competent in their field. Trust is crucial for inspiring others to follow you.

2. **Encourage Creativity in Decision-Making:** Ask your team to think outside the box. There are many creative ways to problem-solve in an organization. Encouraging creative decision-making builds confidence and fosters a sense of responsibility.

3. **Professional Development:** Provide opportunities for team members to grow within your organization through ongoing professional development. Follow up and observe the implementation of newly learned information. Learning new skills allows members to advance in their careers. Ensure individual leadership development plans are tailored to their needs, goals, and aspirations.

4. **Communication:** A work environment where individuals feel free to share ideas, collaborate, and provide feedback without fear of retaliation is essential. One rule I always had was, "All voices will be heard."

5. **Lead by Example:** Transformational leaders always lead by example. It's important for leaders to understand that they are also growing and may need professional development. For example, a leader may excel in collaboration and creativity but fall

short in adaptability and emotional intelligence. Recognize your strengths and areas for growth and be open to further training.

In conclusion, if you want to inspire, motivate, train, or empower team members, transformational leadership is an effective approach to elevate them. Transformational leadership fosters a culture of innovation, communication, collaboration, and creativity. This leadership style drives organizational success and cultivates a sense of purpose for all stakeholders. It's important that leaders recognize the unique gifts within their team members and help them align those gifts with their purpose. Embracing the tenets of transformational leadership enhances individual growth and organizational success.

My goal as a transformational leader was to prepare, empower, and train my team for future leadership roles. My personal vision and mission included empowering others to achieve success, fulfillment, prosperity, and inner peace. When individuals align their gifts with their purpose, they experience a profound sense of fulfillment, leading to a more authentic and meaningful life. This synergy is essential in the workplace, especially when empowering others to lead. The art of Transformational Leadership—encompassing Individual Consideration, Idealized Influence, Inspirational Motivation, and Intellectual Stimulation—empowers individuals to step into leadership greatness and elevate them to new heights. These factors are the epitome of a force multiplier, driving greater success by inspiring and motivating future leaders.

Dr. Theresa A. Moseley

Her Excellency Dr. Theresa A. Moseley is a WOLMI United Nations Peace Ambassador, United States Army Veteran, International Keynote Speaker, 24x Best-Selling Author, 4x International Best-Selling Author, a 3x-Award Winning Educator, and a retired educator after 28 years of service. H.E. Dr. Moseley has been featured in several magazines, including *International Face Magazine*, *Women of Dignity*, *Speakers Magazine*, *Tap-In*, *Vision and Purpose Magazine*, and *The Black Family Magazine*, and has graced the cover of *International Face Magazine*. She has also been featured in over 300 news articles worldwide. H.E. Dr. Moseley delivered a keynote speech at Harvard University with the London Organization of Skills Development. Her Excellency is the 2024 Women of Heart Global International Brand Ambassador.

H.E. Dr. Moseley is the owner and Chief Executive Officer of TAM Creating Ambassadors of Peace LLC, where she provides professional development on Transformational Leadership. Her Excellency uses her signature leadership books, *Step Into Leadership Greatness* Vol 1 and 2, and *Essential Soft Skills for Effective Leadership Steps to Leading With Grace* to train leaders. Her company also provides inspirational and motivational speeches to groups seeking to resolve conflicts in communities, schools, and other organizations aiming to create a peaceful climate and culture. Her Excellency hosts an annual Passion Purpose Peace Summit during International Peace Week. Her mission is to help others find their purpose, leading to success, fulfillment, prosperity, and inner peace. She believes leaders should foster peaceful climates within organizations to establish trust and respect, enhance job satisfaction, increase productivity, and create a healthy workplace.

Embrace, Empower, and Elevate: Three E's for Leadership Success

The Honorable Savannah Winston

Embrace, Empower, and Elevate or synonymous Accept, Inspire, and Lift. It wasn't until very recently that I was reflecting on my leadership journey that I realized that I had to stop running from the call to leadership and fully Embrace MY journey. I am filled with gratitude for the experiences, lessons, and people who have shaped me into the leader I am today. Each step, from starting out as a young girl entrepreneur selling popcorn in my parents' yard to serving as the first black woman Mayor in the 132-year history of my hometown, has been a building block in my leadership story. Embracing leadership requires us to look inward, to accept who we are, where we come from, and where we are going. It's about understanding that leadership is not about perfection but authenticity. To embrace leadership is to accept that we are constantly evolving and that our flaws and imperfections are part of what makes us relatable and effective leaders.

This journey of embracing leadership often begins with self-awareness. It requires us to confront our fears and insecurities, to challenge the narratives we've internalized about who we are and what we're capable of. For me, this meant overcoming the doubts that whispered I wasn't ready or worthy to lead. It meant leaning into my faith and trusting that the skills, experiences, and passions I had been given were no accident. Leadership, I've come to realize, is less about having all the answers and more about having the courage to ask the right questions and take the first step.

As I navigate my unique path, I encourage you to lead with courage, compassion, and conviction, embracing YOUR journey and the transformative power of leadership. A journey is more than just physical movement from one place to another. It represents growth, learning, and transformation. Life itself is a journey, filled with its own set of challenges and triumphs. It is deeply personal, and not everyone will understand the path you choose to walk. Embrace your leadership journeys as uniquely yours, shaped by your faith, values, and lived experiences.

Leadership, in its essence, is about impact and influence. This is where we as leaders can Empower others. Empowerment is a dynamic, evolving process that requires growth, adaptability, and a commitment to continuous learning. Each step of my journey has prepared me to lead with empathy and cultural competence. Engaging with individuals from diverse backgrounds has taught me the value of active listening, open-mindedness, and mutual respect. Leadership in today's interconnected world requires an appreciation for cultural differences and a commitment to creating inclusive spaces where everyone feels valued and heard. Cross-Cultural Competence (3C) has become a central theme in my leadership philosophy. It involves understanding and navigating the complexities of different cultural perspectives while fostering an environment of collaboration and mutual learning. As a reflective leader, I've come to realize that embracing diversity is not just about meeting quotas; it's about leveraging the richness of varied experiences to drive innovation, creativity, and collective success. Culture, with its intricate tapestry of customs, arts, achievements, beliefs, language, norms, and values, plays a significant role in shaping who we are as individuals and leaders.

In elementary school, being one of the few black students in my classes became my norm. While this presented challenges, it also prepared me to navigate diverse environments with resilience and adaptability. Teachers and guidance counselors saw leadership potential in me even when I didn't recognize it myself. These were leaders that first empowered me. To inspire others, a leader must first be inspired. My faith, family, and community have been constant sources of inspiration, fueling my determination to persevere and make a difference. Empowerment is the foundation of impactful leadership. Empowerment is about equipping individuals with the tools, knowledge, and confidence they need to succeed. It involves fostering a sense of ownership and accountability while providing the support and guidance necessary for growth.

Empowerment is a transformative process that enables individuals to recognize their own strengths and capabilities, inspiring them to take bold steps toward their goals. Are you empowered? Are you able to empower others?

Leadership, I've learned, is both a calling and a choice. After high school and college, my journey as a leader expanded into community service. My passion for serving others became the cornerstone of my leadership philosophy. As a servant leader, I sought to prioritize the well-being of people and communities. Community service experience taught me the importance of collaboration, effective communication, and strategic planning. I have developed a profound appreciation for the power of collective action and the strength that comes from uniting diverse perspectives toward a common goal. These are the opportunities to Elevate others. Elevation is about lifting others up. As a leader, I strive to create opportunities for growth and development for those around me. Whether mentoring a young professional, advocating for a community initiative, or empowering a team member to take on a new challenge, my goal is to help others reach their full potential. Elevating others not only strengthens the team but also fosters a culture of trust, respect, and shared success.

My leadership journey took a historic turn when I was elected as the first person of color to serve on the Town Commission in the town's 131-year history. Later, I broke another barrier as the first woman and person of color to serve as President Commissioner or Mayor. These milestones were not just personal achievements but symbols of progress and elevation for my community. To elevate others in leadership is often tested in times of adversity. Reflecting on my journey, I've faced numerous challenges that have shaped me into the leader I am today. From overcoming societal barriers to navigating personal hardships, each obstacle has taught me the importance of resilience, adaptability, and perseverance. Adversity, I've learned, is not a setback but an opportunity for growth and transformation.

One of the most significant lessons I've learned is the power of perspective. Challenges can be daunting, but by viewing them as opportunities to learn and grow, we can turn setbacks into stepping stones to empower and to elevate. As a leader, it is our responsibility to model this mindset for others, demonstrating that with faith, determination, and hard work, anything is possible. It is important to share our stories to inspire and empower others.

To current and aspiring leaders, remember the three E's: Embrace, Empower, and Elevate. Embrace your journey, no matter how unconventional or challenging it may be. Leadership is not a straight path, and the uniqueness of your story is what makes you a powerful leader. By accepting your individuality and the experiences that have shaped you, you lay the foundation for authentic and impactful leadership. Celebrate your culture and the diversity that shapes our world. Each of us carries a rich portfolio of experiences, values, and traditions that contribute to the broader narrative of leadership. Embracing diversity is not just a responsibility; it's an opportunity to learn, grow, and create spaces where everyone's voice is valued.

Strive to inspire others by living your values and leading with integrity. Inspiration often stems from vulnerability—sharing your struggles, triumphs, and lessons learned along the way. When you open up about your journey, you empower others to do the same. Through your actions, you show others that they too have the strength and capability to rise above challenges and reach their potential.

Elevate those around you by creating opportunities for growth and collaboration. Leadership is not about standing alone at the top; it's about building a community where everyone can succeed. Mentorship, active listening, and fostering inclusion are powerful tools for lifting others. When you help others reach their goals, you strengthen the collective impact of your team, organization, or community.

And let me also encourage, three P's for leadership success. Find your Passion. Allow the passion for your vision and goals to drive your work ethic. Your passion shows your commitment and motivation for your success. Your passion will drive you to go the extra mile as a leader. Patience allows leaders to take a step back and view the bigger picture, making well-informed decisions. It takes time and patience to mentor and develop others. Leaders must have perseverance to push through challenges and setbacks. Perseverance shows resiliency and consistency for achieving success. Balancing passion, patience, and perseverance, the three P's, leaders can build trust, inspire growth, and sustain success!

Remember, leadership is a journey, not a destination. It is through this journey that we discover our true potential and purpose. By embracing your path, empowering others, and striving to elevate those around you, you contribute to a legacy of compassionate, inclusive, and transformative leadership. The world needs leaders like us who are willing to take bold steps, inspire change, and leave a positive impact for generations to come.

The Honorable Savannah Winston

The Honorable Savannah Winston is a community leader being the first person of color to be elected to serve as a Commissioner for the Town of Preston, first woman and person of color to serve as President Commissioner "Mayor" for the Town of Preston. Savannah is an accountant, project management professional, entrepreneur, and business owner of VanTech Business Solutions (VTBS) located in Preston offering a portfolio of administrative support services.

Professionally, Savannah Winston has over thirty years of multi-faceted experience in the consulting industry. Her employment history includes being engaged in multiple large-scale projects for major government focused health systems that involved research and data gathering, information system design, testing and training, strategic & project planning, gap analysis, and toolkit development. She currently works as a

Specialist for the Centers for Medicare & Medicaid Services, Center for Program Integrity.

She has earned a bachelor's degree in accounting from the University of Maryland Eastern Shore and has a master's degree in Management Information Systems from Bowie State University. She is currently pursuing a Doctorate degree in Education and Executive Leadership at Bowie State University, 3rd Year Doctoral Executive Fellow. She is also a Class of 2020 graduate of Shore Leadership and 2022 graduate of Shore Leadership 2.0.

Passion, Patience, and Perseverance are the three "P's" that motivates her daily. Savannah's life verse is Proverbs 3:5-6 "Trust in the Lord with all your heart and lean not on your own understanding; In all your ways acknowledge Him and He will direct your path."

Lead With Courage, Lift with Purpose, and Leave a Legacy of Empowerment

Dr. Rhonda M. Wood

"You never know how strong you are until being strong is your only choice." ~ Bob Marley

How it Started

How often do we wear masks to hide our struggles, especially in Corporate America, where expectations of perfection loom? For 25 years, I climbed the corporate ladder with precision, discipline, and unwavering commitment. But behind the accolades, I was fighting a silent battle—mental health challenges that threatened to derail my career and life. This struggle is not unique to me; I share it so others know they are not alone.

Leadership is often romanticized as a position of power, confidence, and certainty. But what happens when your leadership journey forces you to confront your deepest vulnerabilities? For me, leadership was not just about managing teams or delivering results; it became a profound personal journey of resilience, authenticity, and using my story to lift others. Today, as an award-winning global keynote speaker, bestselling author, mental health advocate, and media personality, I stand as a force multiplier, helping others step into their leadership greatness. This is my story of triumph—not despite my mental health struggles, but because of them.

The Corporate Mask

From the moment I entered Corporate America, I was determined to succeed. I worked tirelessly, often clocking 60-hour weeks, climbing the corporate ladder. Promotions and awards followed, and on paper, I was thriving. Yet, internally, I was unraveling. Anxiety and depression would come in waves. I became a master at masking—putting on a brave face during meetings, excelling in presentations, and showing up as the "strong leader" I believed I needed to be.

In truth, I was terrified of being seen as "weak" or incapable. Corporate culture often equates vulnerability with incompetence. I thought I was alone, but as the years passed, I realized my struggles were not unique. Many people were suffering in silence—burnt out, overwhelmed, and desperate for change. I knew I had to be the voice for those who felt unseen and unheard. But first, I had to find my own voice.

The Turning Point

A pivotal moment came when my mental health hit rock bottom. Years of suppressing my struggles led to a breaking point. I remember sitting in my office, staring at my reflection, tears streaming down my face. The person staring back was a shell of the woman I once knew. I realized that if I didn't address my mental health, I would lose everything I had worked for, including myself.

Then, I made a life-changing decision: I would no longer allow fear or shame to define me. I sought therapy, educated myself about mental health, and slowly began to heal. Most importantly, I stopped hiding. I shared my story—first with close colleagues and then with larger audiences. What started as a whisper of truth became a roar of authenticity. As I embraced my struggles, I discovered that vulnerability was not a weakness; it was a superpower. My openness allowed others to step forward, admit their challenges, and seek help. By leading with courage and honesty, I became a force multiplier, empowering those around me to face their fears and rise above them. This courage in vulnerability inspires and empowers others to do the same.

The Leadership Win: Finding Purpose Beyond the Pain

The true turning point in my leadership journey came when I realized my pain had a purpose. I left Corporate America to pursue a calling far greater than any title or paycheck. I became a global keynote speaker, sharing my story on stages around the world. I authored bestselling books that gave others permission to own their truth. I became a media personality, using my platform to amplify messages of hope, resilience, and mental health awareness.

Every stage, every page, every interview became an opportunity to inspire and uplift others. My story resonated because it was real. People saw themselves in my struggles and found hope in my triumphs. I became living proof that it is possible to lead, achieve, and inspire—even when life throws its hardest punches.

The Leadership Lessons

1. **Vulnerability is Your Superpower:** For years, I believed that showing my struggles would make me less credible as a leader. I was wrong. Vulnerability creates connection, trust, and relatability. When I began sharing my story, I found that others were drawn to my authenticity. People do not follow perfection; they follow courage. When you lead with vulnerability, you give others permission to be themselves, fostering a more inclusive and supportive work environment and enhancing your leadership effectiveness.

2. **Your Challenges Can Be Your Catalyst:** The challenges we face are not roadblocks; they are stepping stones. My mental health journey gave me the tools to lead with empathy, compassion, and resilience. Instead of viewing struggles as setbacks, reframe them as opportunities for growth and transformation. For instance, you can use your experiences to connect with your team on a deeper level, fostering a more supportive and understanding work environment. Leaders who have overcome adversity are often the most impactful because they lead from a place of wisdom and strength. This transformation of challenges into opportunities gives others hope and optimism.

3. **Mentorship and Collaboration Multiply Impact:** I did not get here alone. Along my journey, I had mentors who believed in me, encouraged me, and guided me. As a leader, it is your responsibility to pour into others—to share your knowledge, experiences, and opportunities. Collaboration amplifies impact. By investing in others, you elevate them to new heights, creating a

ripple effect of success. This emphasis on mentorship and collaboration makes the audience feel supported and encouraged and helps them realize the power of collective growth and achievement in leadership.

4. **Normalize Mental Health Conversations:** Mental health is as important as physical health, yet it remains taboo in many spaces. As leaders, we must create environments where people feel safe sharing their struggles without fear of judgment. When we normalize mental health conversations, we foster a culture of support, understanding, and wellness, leading to greater success for everyone.

5. **Take Bold Action:** Bold leadership requires bold action. Whether sharing your story, starting a new initiative, or taking a leap of faith, do not let fear hold you back. The world needs leaders who are willing to take risks, break barriers, and pave the way for others. Be unapologetic in your pursuit of purpose.

The Charge

Today, I stand as living proof of what is possible when we lead with courage, authenticity, and a bold approach to life. My journey from surviving to thriving has been filled with challenges, but also with purpose. Through my work as a global keynote speaker, bestselling author, and mental health advocate, I have made it my mission to lift others as I rise—to be a force multiplier who empowers others to step into their leadership greatness.

If there is one message I want to leave you with, it is this: Your struggles do not define you—your response to them does. Leadership is not about perfection; it is about progress. It is about showing up, sharing your story, and using your experiences to create a better world.

So, I challenge you to embrace your journey—the good, the bad, and everything in between. Be bold. Be vulnerable. Be the leader who lifts others to new heights. Because when we rise together, we create a legacy of greatness that lasts.

Last Words

Your leadership journey is not just about you. It is about the lives you touch, the people you empower, and the legacy you leave behind. Step into your greatness and, in doing so, help others discover their own. Lead with courage, lift with purpose, and leave a legacy of empowerment.

Dr. Rhonda M. Wood

Dr. Rhonda M. Wood, an award-winning international keynote speaker, bestselling author, and media personality, is celebrated as a leading voice in mental health advocacy. Her journey, which began in the corporate world, was marked by professional success but also a silent battle with depression, anxiety, and unresolved childhood trauma. Her courageous decision to seek therapy transformed her life, inspiring her to share her mental health journey with authenticity, transparency, and most importantly, resilience. These qualities resonate deeply with women worldwide, inspiring them to face their own challenges with courage.

Dedicated to normalizing mental health conversations, Dr. Wood uses her platform to foster compassion, awareness, and acceptance in addressing mental health challenges. Her warm and empathetic approach resonates with her audience as she amplifies the voices of professional women who struggle in silence through her WBGR media channels. This approach has helped her build a supportive community that thrives on openness and shared healing experiences. Recognized on major networks, including ABC, NBC, CBS, and FOX, Dr. Wood's advocacy has earned her numerous accolades and widespread recognition for her global impact on women's mental health.

Beyond media, Dr. Wood serves on the Board of NAMI Prince George's County, where she plays a pivotal role in influencing policy and outreach in mental health. Her passion for guiding women to reset their values, renew their vision, and rediscover their voices is evident in her advocacy work. She champions the belief that healing begins with breaking our silence and learning to "heal out loud."

Team Building

Naomi Carrington-Hockman

"If you want to go fast, go alone. If you want to go far, go together." ~ African Proverb

One way to step into leadership greatness is by building high-performing teams. I have been required to lead teams of soldiers, government civilians, and defense contractors and have accomplished extraordinary missions. Here are some areas for consideration if you are building a team:

- Determine what you need help with.
- New employee considerations
- Employee retention
- Leading remote teams

Determine What You Need Help With

You cannot be a great leader if you are not surrounded by great employees. When putting together your team, focus on how to get the most out of them. Determine precisely what you need help with. Do you need employees who can take over some of your responsibilities? Or do you need to hire people with expertise you do not currently have? If you find it challenging to know when to expand, these quick tips will tell you it is time:

- Handling big tasks becomes tough because you spend more time on rote work or small details.
- Your customers are not getting enough attention.
- You have a steady stream of work, not just a week or two of intense work.
- You and your current staff are consistently overworked and frustrated.

- You are turning down work because you cannot keep up.
- The need for specialized personnel for specific tasks arises.
- You are making enough money to hire employees.

New Employee Considerations

Hiring new people can be dicey. The uncertainty of a new hire can cause some businesspeople to want to avoid hiring. Bad employees have burned many experienced hiring managers and entrepreneurs, but good workers are ready to support your business—you must find them.

Here are five important things to consider when employing a new employee:

1. Your business culture
2. Character
3. Diversity
4. The type of people you want
5. Your branding

Your Business Culture

Before recruiting new staff, define your business culture. Your company's culture comprises values, traditions, behaviors, attitudes, and beliefs. You do not want to hire people who do not fit your business culture. To maintain the culture and working environment you want, work towards hiring people who will enhance it. Look for people who share your values and understand your brand and company vision.

Character

After defining your business culture, assess the character of the employees or the people you intend to employ. Hire people of strong integrity and character, who are knowledgeable about your products, ethical, and cooperative. This will reduce the possibility of having any bad employee stories.

Hiring trustworthy employees provides a safe working environment and allows you to unburden some of your responsibilities without fear. The aim is to have great team members who will boost productivity, but no employee will be perfect. However, a team member who works with integrity will produce ongoing rewards.

Diversity

The beauty of any team is diversity. With the changes in the business landscape over the past sixty years, many companies have come to understand that diversity is a strength.

If you are planning to bring in people from many demographics, here are a few things you can do:

- Incorporate diversity into your business culture.
- Lay out your criteria before the interview.
- Post your advertisements for job opportunities in different localities.
- Attend job fairs in different communities.
- Start as a diverse group; this makes it easier to continue that way.

Diversity, equity, and inclusion (DEI) is a topical subject. Take the time to understand DEI and incorporate a program that works for your organization, business, and/or team.

The Type of People You Want

You may know exactly what kind of people you want, but how do you find them? To find people, use a variety of avenues; this helps you access a wide range of people.

Try using these avenues:

- Your personal network
- Social media networks
- Online job boards
- The newspaper or physical job boards

Your Branding

When branding, you are not only selling your products; you are also selling your company. When branding, think of creative and engaging ads that will attract people to your business, provide them with a clear idea of your company's ideals, and influence them to either buy from or work for you.

Employee Retention

The Importance of Making Your Employees Feel Valued

You cannot underestimate the power of treating your employees well. The difference you make in their lives is not in how much money they make, but in how you treat them. How you treat your employees often depends more on the company's morale than individual income levels. In the short term, your business may thrive under high-pressure management, and your employees may work twice as hard to meet your rising expectations. However, in the long term, there are significant consequences, which may include:

- Increased health problems among employees, which may be difficult to manage due to high healthcare costs. A study conducted by BMC Public Health concluded that individuals who work at high- to medium-strain jobs visit their general practitioners 26% more than those who work at low-pressure jobs. They also go to a specialist 27% more often.

- Disengagement among employees. This is the second issue that arises from high-pressure management. When employees become less committed to their jobs, it reduces their productivity.

- Lost loyalty is another problem associated with high-stress jobs that eventually leads to high turnover rates. Employees slowly lose interest in their work, leaving them feeling unappreciated and unhealthy.

Today, replacing an employee is expensive and should be avoided when possible.

How Do You Ensure Maximum Retention?

- Compensate Them Well: You do not have to pay your employees so well that you forfeit a healthy budget, but paying a fair wage will go a long way.

- Offer Flexibility: A growing number of employees desire flexibility in their work schedules. Many people are looking for jobs that allow them to work remotely or have the ability to work from home some of the time. They want the freedom to work shifts based on their needs.

- Listen to Your Employees and Show Them You Care: Taking time to listen to the people who work for you will influence how they work and feel about their time at work. As an entrepreneur or boss, do your best to give your employees your undivided attention.

- Show Your Employees Appreciation: Everyone, at some point, needs to feel seen and appreciated. Some personality types need more affirmation than others, but what people want to know is that their work is important and valued.

- Teach Your Employees Well the First Time: When teaching your employees new skills, it is better to teach them well the first time. It may feel like an uphill task, but teaching them well initially is far better than retraining them on the same functions.

- Do not Be Afraid to Loosen Up a Bit: Work is a place of work. However, there is also power in play. For example, Google, one of the most successful tech companies in the world, knows the value of happy employees. They allow employees to bring their pets to work and offer gyms, swimming pools, video games, foosball tables, and many other perks. You may not be able to give your employees as many perks as Google, but you can take a page out of their handbook.

Good Practices for Leading a Remote Team

Remote work has many advantages but can be challenging, especially when trying to run a team. For someone who is not experienced, managing a team from a distance can be difficult. However, certain leadership qualities are effective whether you are working on-site or remotely. These leadership qualities are:

- Good communication skills
- Ability to connect well with team members
- A clear vision and the ability to relay your goals and expectations
- Confidence and humility
- Curiosity and eagerness to learn
- Willingness to be critiqued
- Ability to take smart risks
- Emotional intelligence
- Strategic and innovative

These leadership qualities are essential for leading a team in an office or remotely.

Conclusion

One can step into greatness by placing serious thought and consideration into (1) determining what one needs help with, (2) applying new employee considerations, (3) catering to employee retention, and (4) leading remote teams.

Naomi Carrington-Hockman

Naomi is a world-renowned major transformation expert, international speaker, best-selling author, and philanthropist. Amversatile and proven leader with almost thirty years of military and civilian leadership, decision-making, and management experience. She expertly provides guidance on change and conflict within large organizations and teams. Now semi-retired, Naomi currently works as an IT Defense Contractor.

Always one to give back, Naomi is releasing her new book, "A Major Transformation: 7 Ways to Lead in Any Environment." This book will help seasoned and aspiring leaders learn to stabilize their management seat and put you in charge of your course, maximize your unique potential, unravel the myths and misconceptions about Leadership, discover the challenges that tail transformational leadership and how to overcome them, discover how to master self-discipline for relational and societal gains, learn the best way to lead a team of inspired and dedicated followers, and strategies to earn loyalty, respect, and service.

Naomi earned her Bachelor of Arts in Psychology from Saint John's University, a Master's of Military Arts and Science in Leadership from the US Army Command and General Staff College, a Master of Science in Project Management from Colorado Technical University, and a Project Management Professional Certificate (PMP) from Syracuse University. She is currently completing her Doctor of Information Technology from National University.

Naomi enjoys spending time with her amazing husband and children and has traveled to over 60 countries. She enjoys golfing and scuba diving.

The Leadership Trifecta (Mentorship, Sponsorship, and Coaching)

The Leadership Trifecta: Mentorship, Sponsorship, and Coaching to Shape Future Leaders

Dr. Tilantine Benjamin

From a very young age, I was captivated by reading. Growing up in the inner city of Washington, DC, books were my window to worlds beyond my experience, giving me a sense of adventure and hope. They unlocked endless possibilities. Through reading, I expanded my vocabulary, sharpened my critical thinking, and nurtured my imagination. My love of books introduced me to diverse cultures, unique characters, and extraordinary stories that did more than entertain—they helped me dream big.

Books allowed me to imagine the extraordinary and see myself as part of it. This perspective set the foundation for the big dreams that would shape my life and career. Dreaming big is often where leadership begins. It inspires a vision for the future, a desire to make a difference, and a drive to achieve great things.

The Foundation of Leadership: Dreaming Big

Dreaming big as a child creates the mindset that future leaders need to succeed. It fosters creativity, resilience, and confidence—qualities essential for leadership. When children are encouraged to dream, they begin to see the possibilities, motivating them to pursue ambitious goals.

- Fostering Vision: Big dreams encourage children to imagine a better future. Visionary leaders motivate others with bold ideas and a sense of purpose, which begins with dreaming beyond what is immediately visible.

- Encouraging Problem-Solving: Dreaming big helps children develop creativity and persistence. They learn to find solutions to challenges, a critical skill for effective leadership.

- Building Resilience: The pursuit of big dreams and ambitious goals teaches perseverance. When children face setbacks and keep going, they build resilience.

- Developing Confidence: Dreaming big instills self-belief, empowering children to take risks and trust their ability to make a difference.

- Shaping Purpose: Leadership begins with purpose. Big dreams often connect children to passions or causes they carry into adulthood, influencing their leadership.

- Inspiring Others: When children dream big, they often envision making a difference. Aspirations to create change or help others form the heart of great leadership, and big dreams are often where those aspirations are born.

Reflecting on my journey, I see how dreaming big has shaped my path. Books sparked my imagination, and mentors, sponsors, and coaches helped bring those dreams into reality. Each played a distinct role in my growth, together creating a powerful framework for leadership development—the Leadership Trifecta.

Mentorship: Guiding Growth and Building Confidence

Mentorship is the cornerstone of leadership development. It involves trusted guidance from someone more experienced, offering advice, support, and encouragement. Mentors provide a safe space for reflection, helping mentees build confidence and develop critical skills. Throughout my career, I have been blessed with mentors who poured into me, shaping my journey and enabling me to grow.

Early in my teaching career, I was paired with a mentor who not only guided me through difficult situations but also helped me see my potential as a leader. I recall a conversation where she said, "One day, you'll do this for someone else—and you'll be even better at it." At the time, I couldn't imagine myself in a mentoring role. I was still finding my footing.

The following year, an opportunity arose for me to mentor a colleague. Initially, I hesitated, questioning my experience. But as I worked with my mentee, I recognized many of the same struggles I had faced—self-doubt, uncertainty, and the need for direction. I shared lessons from my journey, both successes and mistakes, and watched as they grew in confidence and capability.

What surprised me most was how much I learned from the process. Mentoring required me to reflect on my leadership style and articulate my decisions. It also deepened my appreciation for my mentors. The most rewarding moment came when my mentee stepped into a leadership role and began mentoring others. Seeing them thrive was a full circle moment—a reminder of how mentoring creates a ripple effect. When we invest in others, we empower them to do the same, building a culture of growth and empowerment.

Sponsorship: Advocating for Visibility and Opportunities

While mentorship focuses on guidance, sponsorship is about advocacy. Sponsors actively champion their protégés, using their influence to open doors and create opportunities. Early in my career, I experienced the transformative power of sponsorship when a colleague went beyond mentoring to advocate for me.

At the time, I was delivering strong results, but my contributions were largely unseen outside my classroom. I didn't realize how much invisibility was limiting my growth until my sponsor stepped in. She recognized my potential and actively advocated for me in meetings I wasn't part of, recommended me for high-profile projects, and connected me with influential leaders. The turning point came when she nominated me for a leadership role I didn't think I was ready for—the countywide Elementary Math Technology Team. Her belief in me was a powerful reminder that sometimes others see our potential before we do.

That opportunity transformed my career and taught me the importance of visibility. Talent and hard work are important, but they must be paired with advocacy to unlock potential. Today, I strive to pay it forward, championing others who might not yet have a seat at the table. Sponsorship isn't just about opening doors—it's about creating a pathway for others to step into their greatness.

Coaching: Driving Accountability and Actionable Growth

Coaching completes the Leadership Trifecta by focusing on self-awareness, accountability, and actionable growth. Unlike mentorship, which is rooted in shared experience, coaching is a structured process that helps individuals identify their goals, overcome obstacles, and develop strategies for success. During a transitional phase in my career, I worked with a coach who helped me uncover blind spots and set clear goals. Rather than providing answers, they asked thought-provoking questions that challenged me to think deeply about my values and priorities.

One pivotal moment came when my coach asked, "Why do you feel the need to say yes to everything?" That question forced me to confront my tendency to equate busyness with worth. With their guidance, I learned to prioritize tasks that aligned with my goals and delegate where possible. This shift improved my productivity and enhanced my leadership by empowering others.

Coaching helped me develop a habit of reflection and intentionality, which continues to shape my leadership style. Growth isn't just about fixing weaknesses—it's about understanding yourself, taking responsibility, and committing to change. Coaching provides the structure and support to make that possible.

The Interconnected Impact of Mentorship, Sponsorship, and Coaching

Mentorship, sponsorship, and coaching are interconnected strategies that together create a powerful framework for leadership development:

- Mentorship builds the foundation by fostering growth, confidence, and readiness.
- Sponsorship opens doors and provides opportunities to apply skills.

- Coaching ensures accountability and equips leaders with the tools to succeed.

Together, these strategies ensure future leaders are prepared to take on challenges, seize opportunities, and inspire others. The impact of the Leadership Trifecta extends beyond individuals. By modeling mentorship, sponsorship, and coaching, we create a culture of support, collaboration, and empowerment.

A Legacy of Leadership

The Leadership Trifecta isn't just about elevating current leaders—it's about inspiring future leaders to dream big. When children are encouraged to dream, they develop the traits that define great leaders: vision, creativity, resilience, and confidence. By fostering these qualities early on, we build a legacy of leadership that empowers individuals to lead with purpose, dream boldly, and make meaningful contributions to the world. Through mentorship, sponsorship, and coaching, we can shape a future where success isn't achieved alone but through the collective support of a thriving community.

Dr. Tilantine Benjamin

Dr. Tilantine Benjamin is a supervisory management analyst with the U.S. Federal Government, where she leads initiatives in leadership development, recruitment, employee recognition, and succession planning to advance human capital goals. A results-driven trailblazer, she has led Lean Six Sigma Black Belt projects that achieved multimillion-dollar cost savings. She has also chaired diversity and wellness councils, spearheading award-winning executive mentorship programs.

Dr. Benjamin began her career as a K-12 educator, earning accolades for her excellence in science, technology, and math instruction, including recognition from a former Maryland governor. She holds degrees from Hampton University, Trinity Washington University, Towson University, and a doctorate from Grand Canyon University, where her dissertation examined the influence of Black Greek-Letter organizations on federal leadership practices.

A best-selling author and certified spiritual life coach, Dr. Benjamin embodies the guiding principle, "Blessed to Be a Blessing." She serves as Executive Director of the Pearls of Wisdom and Educational Resources Foundation and is deeply involved in her community, holding leadership roles in Zeta Phi Beta Sorority, Incorporated, and The Fellowship of Faith Church. Honored with the 2021 Tracey Pinson Trailblazer Award from the African American Federal Executive Association, she remains committed to inspiring others through mentorship, diversity, and philanthropy.

The Transformative Power of Mentorship

Danielle "DJ" Jaeger

Unlocking Your Potential

Have you ever felt that success was just out of reach? As if everyone around you had the key to unlock their potential while you were left on the sidelines? What if the key to your success wasn't a secret at all, but the guidance of someone who had been there before — someone who could see your potential even when you couldn't?

Mentorship is one of the most powerful tools for growth, yet it's often overlooked in the rush of daily life. Mel Robbins shared a profound truth with Oprah Winfrey on her podcast: "Other people never block your way. Only you can do that. Other people lead the way if you allow them to" (Robbins, 30:23). This perspective shaped how I view not only my own career but also leadership itself. Success, I've realized, isn't a finite resource — it's limitless and expands when we empower and uplift others.

This chapter explores the transformative power of mentorship — how it can elevate you professionally and personally, and how, in turn, you can give back by mentoring others. Employees who work with a mentor are promoted five times more often than those without one (Quast, 2011). We'll examine how mentorship fosters empowerment, recognition, and diverse perspectives, as well as helping to overcome imposter syndrome. My journey shows that the path to leadership greatness is one we walk with others by our side.

So, let me ask you: Who is guiding you on your journey, and who are you helping to rise?

My Own Leadership Lesson

Mentorship isn't just a professional buzzword; it's a deeply personal and transformative experience. It's about more than receiving advice or asking for a resume review. It's about being seen, challenged, and empowered to grow into the best version of yourself. My mentorship journey began informally, as a way to navigate uncertainty in my career. But it quickly became a cornerstone of my growth as a leader and an individual.

In my earliest career experience, mentorship became the bridge between doubt and confidence, between limitation and possibility. Through the lessons I learned from mentors — and those I discovered while mentoring others — I embraced diverse perspectives and redefined my pathway to success. Let me share one of the defining moments that shaped my journey.

The Unexpected Mentor

Shortly after I graduated college, I found myself working in a retail store selling electronics; I was part of a large group of sales representatives, but we also had a handful of highly respected electronic repair technicians. I was in my 20s, convinced that hard work alone would lead to a promotion. It's all about how much effort you're willing to put in, right? I immersed myself in every detail of our products, excelled at de-escalating upset customers, trained new employees, provided them coaching feedback, and worked closely with the managers on special initiatives. I thought I was demonstrating my potential as a leader and a key player in the success of the store through the empowerment of my fellow employees.

After six months, I was hand-selected to attend a week-long district-wide electronic repair certification course. I was excited to add a new tool to my belt, but I was also delighted that the managers had recognized my potential. After I was certified, I felt sure a promotion was imminent. Days went by with no calendar invite or email; days turned to weeks, and a few months later I still hadn't heard anything. I thought they had recognized me as a high potential leader, but now I was filled with self-doubt. I felt like I didn't have the keys to unlock my potential, and my performance began to falter. It was then that I received an email from a manager — the subject line was "New Repair Technician Announcement" and everyone in the store was copied.

This was it, my big moment! I couldn't contain my giddiness — I don't think I have ever clicked that quickly to read an email in my life! There in the body of the email I found myself face to face with a smiling photograph of someone who definitely was not me — he had gotten the role that I had been aspiring to. I started to cry and one of my co-workers walking by noticed; she quickly sat down and asked what was going on. She and I had a lot in common and I wanted to be just like her. She was kind, friendly, smart, a peer leader, and although only a few years older than me, she was already a repair technician — seeing a fellow woman succeed in the role I wanted was inspiring, but I also felt some jealousy. What was I missing?

As I wiped my tears, she suggested we take our break together. Once we were out of the store, I started to share that I felt overlooked, and that I didn't understand why I couldn't be a repair technician even after preparing intensively. She then asked which manager I was working with and I met her with a confused look. Nobody was assigned a manager; there were several that cycled with each shift and we all shared them. She smiled and told me the story of her promotion from sales to repair technician. She worked with a single manager to mentor and coach her over a year; she filled skill gaps and made her technician intentions known. Her manager mentor recommended her for stretch projects and shared her big wins with the manger team. This was the support I needed to be promoted — not just wishing and keeping my intentions to myself, but sharing where I wanted to go next, being clear about my goals, and vocal about my achievements.

I gained an unexpected mentor that day; she wanted to see me succeed, gave me feedback, and helped me understand how to change my situation. She shared her story of success that helped me feel less alone.

After my discussion with her, I approached a manger I admired and asked for him to serve as my mentor. He and I worked together for the next year, closing my skill gaps and building my technical expertise, which enabled me to be hired as a repair technician. By making progress toward my goal of promotion and having that progress recognized by my mentor and peers, I restored my self-confidence.

Through the pathway of mentorship, I discovered the key to unlock my potential. I think Mel Robbins said it best, "what we get wrong about the game of life is you're not playing against other people - you're playing with them. And you can learn how to be a better player from other people" (Robbins 31:35). I needed to learn from those around me through mentorship and begin to teach others what I knew in serving as a mentor.

Your Mentorship Journey

Mentorship is more than just a career tool; it's a lifeline to self-discovery and empowerment. Through the challenges and triumphs of my own career journey, I've come to understand that success is never achieved in isolation. It's a collaborative effort fueled by guidance, encouragement, coaching, and shared wisdom. Whether it's the unexpected mentor who helps you through a difficult moment or the formal manager mentor who champions your goals, these relationships create a foundation for growth that's as profound as it is lasting.

Reflecting on my story, I see the power of stepping into my own potential while helping others do the same. I've embraced diverse perspectives, mostly overcome imposter syndrome, and, most importantly, built meaningful connections that have shaped who I am as a leader. Even now, though my mentor network has grown, my unexpected mentor is still someone I turn to for advice. Each promotion, achievement, and opportunity I've had has been a direct result of my network of mentors, and the lessons I learned from those who walked alongside me and showed me the way.

What I've learned is this: mentorship is about clarity and connection. It's about being intentional in articulating your goals and seeking out those who can help you achieve them. It's also about being a force multiplier and elevating those around you to new heights — becoming the person who listens, guides, and celebrates others as they rise. By doing so, we create a ripple effect of empowerment and recognition, shaping a culture where success knows no limits, and nobody gets left on the sidelines.

So, I'll leave you with this: success is abundant, and greatness is multiplied when we uplift and empower one another. Researchers have found that 89% of those who were mentored will also mentor others, indicating a positive cycle of development (Gill & Roulet, 2021). Who can you mentor today? How will you use your own experiences to help others rise? Because when we lead with intention and generosity, we don't just achieve success—we also create it for others.

Works Cited

Gill, Michael, and Roulet, Thomas. "Stressed at Work? Mentoring a Colleague Could Help." Harvard Business Review, 17 Sept. 2021, hbr.org/2019/03/stressed-at-work-mentoring-a-colleague-could-help.

Quast, Lisa. "How Becoming a Mentor Can Boost Your Career." Forbes, Forbes Magazine, 21 Aug. 2012, www.forbes.com/sites/lisaquast/2011/10/31/how-becoming-a-mentor-can-boost-your-career

Robbins, Mel., guest: "How to improve your life with ONE change | Oprah & Mel Robbins." Conducted by Oprah Winfrey, The Oprah Podcast, 10 Dec. 2024, http://pod.link/1782960381

Danielle "DJ" Jaeger

"DJ" Jaeger is a dynamic leader and learning development strategist known for empowering learning professionals, leveraging technology, and designing tailored training solutions. She is a Sr. Training Manager at Akamai Technologies, an Instructional Design professor at Portland State University, and a sought-after public speaker, writer, and mentor with expertise in learning technology and neurodiversity. "DJ" is committed to fostering the next generation of data-driven and inclusive L&D leaders as the Director of Professional Development at ATD Cascadia and creating transformational digital learning experiences for small businesses and non-profits as the founder of Lightbulb Learning.

The Journey to Greatness: A Story of Elevation

Dr. Michelle Boulden-Hammond

When I was younger, I never imagined my life would be about helping others step into their greatness. But here I am, standing in a room filled with eager faces, sharing how I found my purpose in empowering others.

It all started with my journey. I was the person who doubted myself constantly. Every idea seemed too big, every dream too distant. I'd see others succeeding and tell myself they had something I didn't—resources, talent, or luck. I was stuck in a cycle of comparison and self-doubt, unaware that my mindset was the only thing holding me back.

One day, everything changed. A mentor looked me in the eye and said, "You have something powerful inside you, but you're hiding from it. Why?" That question haunted me. Why was I hiding? What was I afraid of? The truth was, I was scared of failing, but even more, I was scared of succeeding and not knowing how to handle it.

I realized I needed to start somewhere, so I took small steps. I invested in personal growth, attended workshops, and surrounded myself with people who believed in possibilities. As I grew, something clicked: the energy and guidance I was receiving could be passed on. I wasn't just meant to grow—I was meant to help others grow too.

The Shift to Helping Others

It began organically. A colleague, overwhelmed with self-doubt about leading a project, came to me. I shared my story and encouraged her, offering strategies to overcome her fear. To my surprise, she succeeded and told me how much my words had shifted her perspective.

That moment sparked something in me. If my small encouragement could inspire her, imagine what intentional effort could do for others. I began diving deeper into understanding how to empower people, not only helping them believe in their potential but also giving them practical tools to act on it.

Building a Framework for Elevation

Over time, I developed a simple framework for helping others elevate to their greatness, which I now live by and share when coaching or mentoring. Let me walk you through it:

1. **Awareness:** The first step is recognizing inner potential. Many are blind to their greatness because they've been conditioned to see only their flaws. I encourage journaling about strengths, accomplishments, and times they've overcome challenges. Reflection builds awareness, the foundation of growth.

Tip: Ask yourself, "What do I consistently do well that others compliment me on?" Often, your strengths are things you take for granted.

2. **Mindset Shift:** Greatness starts in the mind. I've worked with people who had all the skills and opportunities but couldn't move forward due to limiting beliefs. Reframing negative thoughts is powerful. Instead of thinking, "I can't do this," replace it with, "What if I succeed?" That question opens up possibilities.

Tip: Practice daily affirmations. Write statements like, "I am capable of achieving my dreams," and say them aloud every morning.

3. **Clarity of Vision:** You can't elevate if you don't know where you're going. I guide people to gain clarity on their goals. It's not enough to say, "I want to be successful." What does success look like? Is it financial freedom? A thriving business? Time to travel? Define your vision to create actionable steps to achieve it.

Tip: Break big goals into smaller milestones. For example, if you want to start a business, your first step might be researching your industry, then developing a business plan.

4. **Taking Action:** Here's where most get stuck: the fear of starting. I always say, "Start messy, but start." It doesn't have to be perfect; it just has to be done. One client wanted to write a book but spent years waiting for the perfect idea. I challenged her to write one

page a day, no matter how messy. Six months later, she had a completed manuscript.

Tip: Set a timer for 15 minutes and work on your goal without distractions. You'll be amazed at what you can accomplish in small bursts.

5. **Consistency:** Elevation doesn't happen overnight. It's the result of showing up daily, even when it's hard. I teach people to build habits that align with their goals. Consistency builds momentum, and momentum creates transformation.

Tip: Use habit trackers to stay accountable. Mark an "X" on your calendar every day you work toward your goal.

6. **Celebrate Wins:** Finally, I emphasize celebrating progress. Too often, people focus on what they haven't achieved instead of acknowledging how far they've come. Every small win matters, and celebrating them builds confidence.

Tip: At the end of each week, write down three things you're proud of. This practice shifts your focus to positivity.

Watching Others Rise

One of my proudest moments came a few years into this work. I was coaching Elena, who dreamed of launching her nonprofit but felt she lacked the experience and confidence to lead. We worked through her limiting beliefs, defined her vision, and created a plan. Slowly, Elena stepped into her greatness. She secured funding, built a team, and launched her nonprofit, now supporting hundreds of families.

Watching her journey reminded me why I do this work. It's not just about helping someone achieve a goal; it's about witnessing the ripple effect of their greatness. When Elena stepped into her power, she changed her life and the lives of the people her nonprofit serves.

The Challenges of Elevating Others

This work isn't always easy. Some resist change, clinging to comfort zones. Others are paralyzed by fear or self-doubt. In those moments, I've learned to be patient and compassionate. Elevation is a journey, and everyone moves at their own pace.

I also remind people that setbacks are part of the process. Failure doesn't mean you're not capable; it means you're learning. I share my failures openly, showing others that it's possible to rise after falling.

Final Thoughts and Parting Tips

Greatness is within all of us. It's not reserved for the lucky or privileged. It's not about being perfect or having all the answers. It's about believing in your potential, taking action, and refusing to give up.

If you're reading this and wondering how to help someone else elevate, start by being a mirror. Reflect their potential back to them. Ask what they dream of and why they're holding back. Share your journey, because vulnerability inspires connection. Above all, remind them that they are worthy of greatness—not because of what they do, but because of who they are.

Remember: when you help someone rise, you rise too. Greatness isn't a solo journey—it's a shared one. Together, we can create a world where everyone steps into their power and lives a life they're proud of.

Now, go out there and elevate someone. Because the world needs more greatness, and it starts with you.

Dr. Michelle Boulden-Hammond

Dr. Michelle Boulden- Hammond Author/Singer /Songwriter / Personal Growth Coach is a versatile individual adept at navigating her faith, marriage, business, and professional relationships with a unique blend of inspiring and coaching skills. Hailing from Talbot County, MD, she originates as a small-town country girl but has surmounted numerous life challenges, including birth defects, low self-esteem, rejection, and mental abuse.

She has received her PhD from Holistic Professionals of Color University and leads as one of the professors at this prestigious school advocating for those of the BIPOC community worldwide. Graduating with a Master of Arts in Human Services in Counseling from Liberty University and possessing a CLC Certificate from the International Coaching Federation, Michelle incorporates her diverse skill set into her coaching practice. She is community and collaborative for leadership within her community. Renowned for her charismatic personality, she empowers individuals to surpass their current limitations and strive for more. She has been married to her husband Elvis for 29 years and loves her family, two children and five grandchildren.

Purposeful Leadership

The Force Within: The Foundation to Elevating Others

Tamera P. Jones

"Leadership is the capacity to *influence* others through *inspiration*, generated by *passion*, motivated by *vision*, birthed from *conviction*, produced by *purpose*."[1] ~ Dr. Myles Munroe

Leadership is often viewed as holding a title or position, directing others, or serving as the face of a group. However, true leadership transcends titles or roles. It starts with recognizing the *force within*—your unique gifts, talents, convictions, and passions—and using them to uplift others.

Serving, impacting, and influencing others for the greater good are key qualities of a leader. This is the essence of being a **force multiplier**: someone who elevates those around them, amplifies their potential, and creates a ripple effect of success that benefits everyone.

So, the question becomes: *Are you willing to step into your unique purpose and become a force multiplier, elevating others to new heights?*

The Force Within: Leadership Rooted in Purpose

Purpose is the compass of true leadership. It provides clarity, conviction, and courage to inspire and elevate others. It's the driving force behind impactful leadership.

From an early age, I felt the pull of purpose. Born three months premature, weighing just 2 pounds and 4 ounces, I defied the odds. My existence felt like evidence of a higher calling—a mission uniquely designed for me. As I grew, my passion for encouraging others and my natural leadership ability became undeniable.

Over time, I realized these gifts were not just personality traits; they were tools for making a lasting impact. However, I discovered an essential truth: before elevating others, I had to invest in my growth. Leadership begins with self-discovery—understanding who you are and aligning with your God-given purpose.

Identifying my purpose allowed me to harness my inner strengths and inspire those around me. This journey of discovering the *force within* was shaped by personal growth, self-reflection, and the influence of leaders who modeled service with integrity and empowerment.

To elevate others, you must first develop yourself and unlock your potential. My journey taught me that embracing my gifts and aligning with God's purpose is the foundation for truly making a difference. The same is true for you—whether you're already leading or just beginning to explore your potential.

Moment of Reflection: Your gifts and experiences are not accidental; they're intentional building blocks for your purpose.

The Power of a Mother's Leadership

My first and greatest influence in leadership was my mother—a woman of faith, integrity, and strength. She raised two children while women were just beginning to enter male-dominated fields. Despite the odds, she returned to college full-time, earned a Bachelor of Science degree in Accounting in less than four years, and worked tirelessly to provide for our family.

She consistently faced challenges head-on, guided by a simple yet profound principle: "Do the right thing, because it's the right thing to do." This unwavering standard shaped my character and approach to leadership.

The hallmark of my mother's leadership was service. She mentored others, encouraged them to take on greater responsibilities, led with confidence, and emphasized "passing it on." My mother taught me that leadership is about lifting others and creating opportunities for them to grow and lead.

Lessons from Corporate America

Working for Fortune 500 companies, I experienced a range of leadership styles. Early in my career, I participated in a financial development program designed to train and mentor future finance leaders. The program was rigorous, combining classroom learning, rotational work assignments, and special projects.

During one assignment, I reported to a manager who provided little guidance and was often absent during critical deadlines. While frustrating, the experience cultivated resilience and resourcefulness. It also reminded me that true leadership isn't defined by titles but by the ability to rise above challenges and inspire others.

Later, a pivotal moment came when I worked closely with a CFO and Director of Global Finance. Recognizing my passion for reading, he gifted me *Who Moved My Cheese?*[2] by Spencer Johnson. This gesture challenged me to embrace change and take bold action. Within a year, I left corporate America to pursue entrepreneurship.

Leadership often requires taking risks, but those risks are intentional steps driven by a desire to realize your full potential. The leadership lessons I gained in corporate America became a springboard for me to realize my potential as a leader and cultivate leadership potential in others.

Moment of Reflection: Challenges and obstacles are opportunities to sharpen your vision and deepen alignment with your mission.

Becoming a Force Multiplier: Leadership Beyond Titles

Leaving my corporate career to pursue entrepreneurship was a bold decision that aligned with my purpose. Taking this leap allowed me to lead in new and meaningful ways.

Entrepreneurship taught me the true meaning of being a force multiplier. My first business, an event planning company, enabled me to create experiences that brought people together. This led to a decade-long career in direct sales—a business model rooted in duplication and teamwork—that helped me refine my leadership skills.

As one of the foundational independent consultants, I played a key role in building the company's #1 sales organization. By coaching, mentoring, recognizing achievements, and empowering others, hundreds of individuals unlocked their potential, creating a ripple effect that inspired thousands.

Great leaders recognize and leverage the strengths of others, empowering them to maximize their gifts for the benefit of the entire group or organization. Leadership isn't measured by personal achievements alone; it's defined by the ability to uplift and inspire others to succeed. When you invest in others, you amplify their potential and expand your own.

While leading a large team, I prioritized one-on-one coaching and mentorship. One individual, in particular, struggled with low confidence and a lack of direction. After months of guidance and support, they rediscovered their confidence and began leading others.

Purposeful leadership requires a shift in perspective—from focusing solely on personal accomplishments to investing in the growth of others. When we empower those around us, we multiply our collective success and impact. As the saying goes, "**T**ogether, **E**veryone **A**chieves **M**ore."

Moment of Reflection: When you empower others to succeed, you amplify not only their growth but also your own.

Building a Legacy of Purposeful Leadership

In 2023, I launched *Beautifully Bold Women*™, a faith-based community designed for women seeking connection, support, and alignment with their God-given purpose. This community reflects my calling to create a space where women can maximize their potential, lead with intention, and make a meaningful impact. Many women have expressed that our community is a place they've been "searching for a very long time," offering opportunities for collaboration and elevating their leadership.

Beautifully Bold Women™ serves as an "incubator" for holistic growth—spiritual, mental, physical, and financial—equipping individuals for leadership greatness. It is a platform for developing, mentoring, and multiplying leaders. Through resources, strategies, and mentorship, we empower women to step boldly into their purpose, fostering transformation that reaches their families, workplaces, communities, and beyond. Together, we are building a legacy of empowered leaders who inspire collective success.

Leadership Lessons to Elevate Others to New Heights

Over the years, I've gleaned powerful leadership lessons to inspire and elevate others. From my experiences shared here, I want to pass on these lessons to you:

- **Leadership begins within:** Focus on self-discovery and align with your God-given purpose to inspire and uplift others.

- **Serve First:** Leadership is an act of service. Prioritize the needs of others, focusing on their growth and success. Find ways to contribute and uplift others.

- **Embrace Change:** Adaptability is key to leadership. Embrace challenges as opportunities to grow and remain resilient and resourceful.

- **Mentor and Empower:** Great leaders multiply their impact by mentoring, supporting, and empowering others.

- **Build Communities:** Foster spaces for connection, collaboration, and growth where people can thrive collectively.

To be a **force multiplier**, you must first embrace the *force within*—your unique gifts, talents, convictions, and passions rooted in your purpose—it's the foundation for elevating others. Purposeful leadership begins with self-awareness and extends outward to inspire growth, success, and transformation in those around you.

Reflect on your journey. Who can you uplift, mentor, or inspire today? The world needs leaders who step boldly into purpose, serve with integrity, and inspire collective success.

Leadership is more than a title; it's a way of being—a commitment to uplift, inspire, and lead with purpose.

The world is waiting.

Now, it's your turn!

Take the next step.

[1] Munroe, Myles. *Becoming A Leader: How to Develop and Release Your Unique Gifts* (New Kensington, PA: Whitaker House, 2018), 33.

[2] Johnson, Spencer. *Who Moved My Cheese?: An Amazing Way to Deal With Change in Your Work and in Life*. New York, Putnam, 1998

Tamera P. Jones

Tamera P. Jones is a transformative coach, speaker, mentor, author, and faith-driven leader passionate about empowering women to master money and live with purpose.

With a mission to inspire spiritual, personal, and financial growth, Tamera helps women gain clarity, confidence, and control to align with their God-given purpose - achieving true freedom and success.

Tamera's professional background includes over 11 years of corporate experience in business and finance, working with Fortune 500 companies as a Business, Financial, and Joint Venture Analyst. For 15 years, she has pursued an entrepreneurial path, building her personal brand and excelling in the direct sales industry as a former independent consultant, national expansion leader, top executive vice president, and foundational leader of the company's #1 sales organization.

As Managing Partner of TPJ World, LLC, Tamera provides coaching, consulting, and training to empower women with the strategies, tools, and accountability needed to transform their relationship with money and reclaim their purpose for intentional, joyful living. She is also the Founder of BUILDMYBANK® and Beautifully Bold Women™, a faith-based community.

Tamera has authored two impactful books: Pain to Purpose: Unleash the Power to Press Through Life's Obstacles and The Unstoppable You!: Success Is Inevitable to the One Who Is UNSTOPPABLE.

Committed to fostering personal growth and building a supportive, God-centered community, Tamera's work helps women thrive in every area of life.

Connect with Tamera:

Website: www.tamerapjones.com

Email: hello@tamerapjones.com

Facebook: @tamerap.jones

Instagram: @iamtamerapjones

LinkedIn: https://www.linkedin.com/in/tamera-p-jones-9689641b/

Vision, Mindset, and Growth

Leadership: A Call to Serve and Transform

Dr. Adebola Ajao

Leadership is more than a role; it is a calling—a calling to serve humanity with vision, courage, empathy, stewardship, and adaptability. True leaders inspire, empower, motivate, and serve, all while fostering an environment where kindness, respect, fairness, and empathy thrive. Answering this call requires a profound love not just for the work but for the people who benefit from it.

Leadership by Example

As the first of five children, I learned early the importance of leading by example. My parents emphasized education and excellence, setting a standard I carried into every space. Their relentless pursuit of excellence and emphasis on character and discipline were constant reminders that leadership starts with self-awareness and personal integrity. This foundation instilled in me the belief that leadership is not about commanding but about inspiring others through actions and achievements.

From childhood, I was conscious of the responsibility that came with having younger siblings who looked up to me. Every action reflected the values instilled in me, and I knew my behavior set the tone for those who followed. These lessons became the bedrock of my approach to leadership, ensuring that I remain an example in all spheres of influence.

Lessons from an Immigrant Experience

At 17, I immigrated alone from Nigeria to the United States for college, embarking on a journey that tested my resilience and adaptability. I remember arriving in West Lafayette, Indiana, in winter, greeted by snow and an unfamiliar culture. Yet, the warmth of the international student office at Purdue University stood out. They demonstrated leadership by creating a supportive environment, assigning peer navigators to help new students transition.

This experience taught me that leadership transcends titles and roles; it is about creating spaces where people feel seen, heard, and supported. The international student office's commitment to ensuring newcomers felt welcome was a testament to the power of mission-driven leadership. Though I never met the office head, their vision and values were evident in every interaction I had with the team. Today, I strive to replicate this environment in every professional and business setting I lead.

The Power of Vision in Leadership

My early career in HIV research and prevention during the HIV/AIDS pandemic was a defining moment. Through the U.S. President's Emergency Plan for AIDS Relief (PEPFAR), I witnessed the transformative impact of vision-driven leadership. Millions of lives were saved and improved, particularly in Africa, through access to quality prevention and treatment services.

This experience reinforced that leadership is about service and vision. It inspired me to pursue greater impact as a public health leader, returning to graduate school at 30 as a young mother. The journey was challenging, stretching me beyond my limits, but it laid the foundation for my future in public health and leadership. It also taught me that leadership requires a willingness to sacrifice comfort for the greater good. The decision to return to school wasn't easy, but it was necessary for me to grow and fulfill my potential as a leader.

Overcoming Challenges as a Leader

After completing my doctoral training, I achieved my dream job as a pharmacoepidemiologist. However, five years into the role, I felt unfulfilled and stagnant. As a minority female scientist, I faced unique challenges navigating a large organization with few senior leaders of color. I worked tirelessly to gain visibility, but this often led to burnout.

This period of struggle became a turning point. I realized challenges are opportunities for self-reflection and growth. I began a personal development journey, discovering my strengths, embracing risks, and giving myself grace to grow. This journey marked the beginning of my leadership evolution.

I learned that leadership is not about fitting into predefined molds but about authenticity. Embracing who I am—a multi-dimensional individual with unique talents, skills, and experiences—allowed me to redefine my approach to leadership. This shift was transformative, enabling me to lead with confidence and authenticity.

Empowering Others Through Leadership

Publishing my book, *Empowered Woman: Five Principles for Living Your Best Life and Fulfilling Your Potential*, was a pivotal moment in my leadership journey. The book outlines principles that transformed my life— Thinking Big, Conquering Your Fears, Finding Knowledge, Finding Mentors, and Taking Action.

Inspired by these principles, I founded Empowering Initiatives, a platform dedicated to equipping women to discover their passion, fulfill their potential, and leave impactful legacies. Since its establishment in 2022, the organization has made significant strides in empowering women, particularly those of African descent in the diaspora.

Through mentorship, networking, and professional development events, we've connected over 200 women, fostering collaboration and mutual support. Topics ranging from personal branding to financial literacy and leadership development have created a supportive ecosystem for professional and business growth.

Empowering Initiatives also prioritizes social responsibility. Ten percent of our book proceeds fund female entrepreneurs in Nigeria, providing seed money to expand their businesses. Witnessing the transformative impact of these funds has been deeply fulfilling. Additionally, our million-book donation project and partnerships with other organizations extend our reach, offering free resources to women at empowerment events.

Building a Legacy of Leadership

Leadership is a continuous journey of growth and service. Through webinars, workshops, coaching, and community-building, Empowering Initiatives equips women with tools to excel professionally and in business. Our vision is to nurture a network of empowered women who maximize their potential and positively impact their communities.

Lessons from the Journey

Leadership requires resilience and adaptability. Whether navigating the challenges of graduate school as a young mother or overcoming barriers as a minority scientist, every experience has shaped me into the leader I am today.

Another critical lesson is the importance of collaboration. Empowering others isn't about imposing one's ideas but about creating platforms where diverse voices can thrive. The success of Empowering Initiatives is a testament to the power of collective effort and shared vision.

Encouraging the Leader in You

As I continue this journey, authenticity, consistency, and leading by example remain at the core of my leadership philosophy. There is a leader in each of us, waiting to emerge. I encourage you to reflect on your passions, identify how you can serve, and embrace your unique calling to lead.

Leadership is not confined to titles or roles; it is about inspiring change, serving with integrity, and creating spaces where others can thrive. Whether in our personal lives, careers, or communities, answering the call to leadership can transform not just those we serve but also ourselves. Embrace the journey, honor your gifts, and lead with vision and purpose. The world needs your leadership.

By embodying the principles of leadership, we can leave a legacy that uplifts others and fosters lasting change. Let your life and work reflect the values of service, empathy, and excellence, inspiring those around you to rise to their highest potential.

Dr. Adebola Ajao

Dr. Adebola Ajao is a pharmacoepidemiologist, author, speaker, personal, professional, and leadership development coach, wife, and mother. She received her Doctor of Philosophy in Epidemiology, a master's degree in public health, and a Bachelor of Science in Biology with a minor in Psychology. Dr. Ajao has dedicated over a decade to protecting public health and advancing women's health through drug safety research and effective drug regulation.

Dr. Ajao is also the founder of Empowering Initiatives, an organization that empowers professional women to identify their passion, walk in their purpose, maximize their impact, and fulfill their highest potential. Dr. Ajao published her first book, Empowered Woman, in 2021, inspired by her journey to empower and transform ordinary women into extraordinary. She is also the co-author of The Habits Code, a collection of success mindsets, habits, and stories, and Grit and Grace: Women Redefining Leadership, a compelling collection of stories of women who embody the perfect blend of grit—the unwavering perseverance to overcome obstacles—and grace—the poise and empathy that define true leadership. Dr. Ajao has also been featured in multiple national and international magazines including New York Weekly, Women's Herald, Women's Journal, CEO Weekly, Readers House Magazine and Entrepreneur Prime.

Through her speaking, workshops, and coaching programs, Dr. Ajao teaches her five growth principles— "Thinking Big," "Conquering Your Fears," "Seeking and Acquiring Knowledge," "Finding Mentors," and "Acting and Following Through"—as practical, easy-to-adopt tools to equip and elevate women personally and professionally.

Criticism to Confidence: A Journey to Leadership

Mary E. Cary

Some leaders use unconventional techniques, yet they are impactful in developing others. As humans, we aren't usually attracted to those who point out our shortcomings or make us feel uneasy. We are drawn to those who praise our successes. Our innate nature gravitates toward leaders we like, who reward and challenge us to become better versions of ourselves. We are motivated and inspired by leaders who recognize and make us feel valued, not those who point out our mistakes.

One of my most memorable leaders was a woman who recruited me from another office within our organization. She believed I had a skillset essential to her team. I was excited to contribute my expertise. However, once I began working for her, she became one of the most critical people I had ever encountered. She scrutinized every detail, down to how I dotted my "i's" and crossed my "t's." She challenged me, particularly my work products, often not privately. Eventually, I became uncomfortable and hesitant about contributing, even though I knew I had the right solution.

A few days before she retired, she called me into her office. She told me she had been hard on me because she saw something great in me. She continued, saying no one took the time to develop her, and her leadership style was developed through trial and error. However, she saw potential and believed in me; therefore, she felt obligated to be rigid and impart things that would help shape me into a better version of myself. My manager said confidently that my career would propel me to an executive position before retirement. Importantly, during my time working for her, she never stopped positioning me for opportunities I otherwise would not have been given. After this conversation, I realized her toughness and critiques were for my development, never meant to tear me down. Her open and honest conversation helped me improve in many areas, ultimately beginning my preparation for leadership.

Yes, this experience was uncomfortable, but it ignited something within me. I was inspired to become a leader who brings out the best in others. It helped me understand the importance of cultivating resiliency and consistency. My awareness and understanding of the significance of truly hearing and recognizing value sharpened, and my confidence increased. I began to focus on my strengths, weaknesses, and desires. My desire to become a leader was ignited. It started with recognizing the importance of introspection and self-awareness. I directed my energy toward the work needed to reach the next level instead of allowing this experience to sabotage my career.

Vocabulary.com defines introspection as "the contemplation of your own thoughts and desires and conduct, self-contemplation, self-examination."[1]

Cultivating self-awareness and understanding who we are helps us identify areas for improvement, a crucial element of personal growth. We become more aware of our emotions and better equipped to manage them. We also learn to recognize our strengths and weaknesses, essential for progress. Self-awareness enhances decision-making and is beneficial when seeking development opportunities to achieve our goals.

Effective leaders help individuals and teams identify personal growth options and future leadership opportunities to gain support and commitment. They help others see the bigger picture. A force multiplier instills teamwork and empowerment and does not use techniques perceived to tear down; instead, they build up and correct when needed. Instead of focusing on people, they focus on the situation. The feedback given is positive and used to provide clarity and answers. Force multipliers use these opportunities to encourage and motivate because they understand their value. They intentionally bring out the best in individuals and teams, understand the importance of helping others pause, and recognize what they need to reach their full potential.

Force multiplier leaders' strengths include fostering trust and building collaborative relationships, making team members feel safe and secure.

They value and embrace diversity in people and perspectives and foster a growth mindset within their teams. Leaders inspire a shared vision and strengthen connections among team members. They actively coach, mentor, and offer growth opportunities that benefit personal and team development. They work to enhance individual and team skills, critical thinking, and leadership potential. Force multipliers prioritize developing other leaders and recognize that providing a safe space is necessary. They support and empower individuals and teams to grow, thrive, and embrace new opportunities outside their comfort zones. They provide the guidance needed to achieve goals and guide them as they learn to make mindset shifts. Leaders who empower others should never feel intimidated by those they mentor. Instead, they should celebrate their successes, support them as they grow, and strive to help them thrive. Encourage those you lead to explore options out of their comfort zones and embrace new challenges. Always be ready to provide support and guidance to help others achieve their goals and shift their mindsets.[2]

People often seek to connect with the human aspect of those they follow, making it crucial to present our authentic selves in every situation. Also, I believe in treating others the way I want to be treated. As a leader who aims to amplify the strengths of those around me, I've learned how vital transparency is. Therefore, I share my experiences, challenges, successes, and the steps I took to become an effective leader. I feel a sense of responsibility to invest in and assist with developing future leaders because my experiences and the lessons I have learned will inspire and assist in cultivating and developing many to become who they were created to be. People matter, and in my experience, I effectively prioritize the needs of others over my own; this does not imply I neglect self-care, but I acknowledge the importance of nurturing and developing others to help them envision greater possibilities. It's my opportunity to give back and prepare to pass the baton.

My approach has been to be transparent and share my experiences, challenges, and wins to show others they can succeed and take accountability for their destiny, even when it seems complicated. Life experiences can be challenging to understand, yet they are often rewarding and valuable to others.

In summary, here are some steps to help develop leaders reach new heights:

- Prioritize encouragement to boost their confidence.
- Remind them what leadership is: influence, empowering others, being themselves.
- Assist individuals and teams in overcoming obstacles they may face.
- Teach them the value of a growth mindset, which helps them recognize that progress is as significant as outcomes.
- For those with self-imposed beliefs about their potential to lead, share examples of other leaders who felt the same way.
    - Remind them they can be themselves and do not have to be like anyone else.
    - Inform them that anyone can lead and help identify associated training.
- Let them know they don't have to do it alone.
    - Identify a coach and/or mentor.
    - Help them see the big picture and how they can impact those around them.

---

[1] Introspection. "Vocabulary.com Dictionary, Vocabulary.com, https://www.vocabulary.com/dictionary/introspection. Accessed. 15 Dec. 2024

[2] Leadership Development. https://www.justinflunder.com/solutions/leadership-development

Mary E. Cary

Mary E. Cary, CEO of Beyond Dimensions, a faith-based coaching and consulting service, is a credentialed personal growth and leadership coach. She is recognized for her remarkable ability to connect with clients and inspire them to unlock their fullest potential. With her infectious enthusiasm and steadfast belief in people, she empowers clients to "SOAR" and reach new heights.

Mary is dedicated to helping clients discover and embrace their unique strengths and capabilities. She drives meaningful transformation in their personal and professional lives through personalized strategies designed to meet each client's specific needs.

Mary served over 30 years in the federal government, holding executive leadership positions in aviation security operations and human resources.

She was a member of the Senior Executive Service, and her accomplishments were recognized with numerous awards. She holds a Master's degree in Psychology (with an emphasis on Life Coaching), a Bachelor's degree in Liberal Studies, and a Bachelor's degree in Religious Studies. Her exceptional leadership experience and knack for engaging in meaningful conversations have earned her clients' appreciation. Additionally, Mary owns a notary practice, providing notarial services and conducting loan signings for mortgage and title companies.

Coaching Philosophy: Reaching your highest potential means understanding who you were created to be and doing the work. It's never too late to grow.

Email: marycary@beyondimensions.org

Facebook: www.facebook.com/me2cary2-10553157457

LinkedIn: www.linkedin.com/in/mary-cary-psy-m-634234b0

Building Bridges: The Power of Connection

Dr. Nadia Monsano

Leadership is not just about personal success; it is about empowering others to rise and fulfill their potential. I experienced this truth firsthand when I coached a client, guiding her through launching her own coaching business—a journey that ultimately led her to run a successful marketing company.

Two years ago, I met Sarah, a passionate entrepreneur with a dream of owning her own marketing company but she was not clear on the roadmap. She envisioned creating a coaching and marketing business to help small businesses thrive but lacked the structure and strategy to get started. Her enthusiasm was contagious, and I saw incredible potential in her when she explained her vision to me.

I offered my business coaching and personal development services to her. With no hesitation, she accepted my offer. From our very first coaching session, I knew that my role extended beyond sharing business strategies; I needed to step into leadership—a space where guidance, patience, and inspiration intersect.

Our coaching process began with defining her business vision. We spent countless hours refining her brand identity, developing a marketing strategy, and crafting service packages that aligned with her strengths. I taught her how to conduct market research, analyze competitors, and create a customer-focused business model.

But the technical know-how was only half the battle. I also focused on mindset coaching—helping her overcome imposter syndrome, build resilience, and adopt a success-oriented mindset. Leadership, after all, involves inspiring belief in oneself and cultivating the same belief in others. Sarah followed every direction with determination. She built her website, launched a content marketing campaign, and networked tirelessly. There were moments of doubt and frustration, but she remained coachable and resilient. I realized that true leadership in coaching involves empowering someone to own their journey while providing unwavering support.

The journey was far from smooth. There were sleepless nights when she questioned her abilities and feared she might fail. Self-doubt often crept in, whispering that she wasn't good enough or experienced enough. We tackled these challenges head-on through coaching sessions focused on overcoming limiting beliefs and building her confidence.

She learned to see failures as learning opportunities rather than setbacks. With every difficult client interaction or marketing campaign that didn't go as planned, she gained valuable insights that strengthened her business acumen. Today, she leads a thriving marketing company with a team of dedicated professionals, proving that perseverance and the right support system can turn fears into triumphs. Her efforts paid off. Within six months, she gained her first coaching clients. A year later, her business expanded into marketing consultancy, reflecting her growing expertise and confidence. Today, she leads a thriving marketing company with a team of dedicated professionals.

This experience reaffirmed that leadership is not about creating followers—it's about creating more leaders. As a coach, my mission was to equip Sarah with the skills and mindset she needed to succeed independently. Leadership in coaching is about seeing potential where others see uncertainty, providing a vision when the path seems unclear, and guiding someone until they can navigate on their own. It's about being patient when progress is slow and celebrating when success finally comes.

One quote that resonates deeply with this journey comes from John Quincy Adams:

"If your actions inspire others to dream more, learn more, do more, and become more, you are a leader."

Coaching Sarah was more than a business endeavor—it was a leadership experience that reminded me how transformative guidance can be. Her success is not just hers; it's a shared triumph born from collaboration, trust, and mutual respect.

As we navigate our professional lives, it's essential to recognize that leadership is not confined to job titles or organizational roles. It manifests in how we mentor, coach, and uplift those around us. Society thrives when leaders step forward—not to command, but to inspire.

Leadership is a legacy we create through the lives we touch and the dreams we help realize. Whether you are a coach, a teacher, or a mentor, remember that your influence can spark extraordinary transformations. When a leader sparks extraordinary transformation in others, the effects can be profound and far-reaching. Clients who experience such change often gain clarity, confidence, and the courage to pursue ambitious goals. They move from uncertainty to empowerment, developing skills they never imagined possible. Their newfound success often extends into their personal lives, strengthening relationships and fostering a positive mindset.

This transformation can create a ripple effect, where those who are empowered become leaders themselves, inspiring others in their circles. Businesses flourish, communities grow stronger, and innovation thrives. Leaders who ignite this kind of change set in motion a cycle of growth that continues long after their direct involvement ends.

By embracing leadership, we can empower others to reach heights they never imagined, creating a ripple effect that extends far beyond our immediate circles. In this interconnected world, the impact of genuine leadership is limitless—and its necessity, undeniable. However, if we choose not to use our leadership skills to help others, the consequences can be equally far-reaching—but in the opposite direction. Opportunities for growth may be lost, potential can remain unrealized, and individuals may continue to struggle in isolation. Businesses can get stagnate, communities may weaken, and innovation could be stifled. When leaders hold back their guidance, the ripple effect of empowerment is replaced by a cycle of missed chances, untapped talent, and diminished progress.

Leadership is not just a privilege—it's a responsibility that shapes the future in powerful ways.

I would like to leave you with Five Steps to Develop Other Leaders

1. **Model Excellence:** Lead by example through integrity, dedication, and consistent performance.

2. **Provide Mentorship:** Offer regular feedback, coaching, and development opportunities.

3. **Encourage Initiative:** Empower others to take ownership of projects and make decisions.

4. **Foster Collaboration:** Create a culture of shared learning and team support.

5. **Celebrate Growth:** Recognize and reward progress, no matter how small, to build confidence and motivation.

As this chapter closes, remember that the impact of leadership extends far beyond what we can see. Every piece of knowledge you share, every bit of guidance you provide, and every moment of support you offer creates ripples of positive change. Step boldly into your role as a leader—whether in your community, your profession, or your personal life. Your influence has the power to uplift, transform, and inspire others to become leaders in their own right. In doing so, you contribute to a world where potential is realized, dreams are pursued, and success is shared.

Dr. Nadia Monsano

In the bustling world of entrepreneurship and relentless pursuit of excellence, Dr. Nadia Monsano stands out as a towering figure of inspiration and innovation. Dr. Nadia is an accomplished 10-time international bestselling author, marketing and branding specialist, and a retired veteran staff sergeant with 10 years of service in the US Army. During her time in the military, Dr. Monsano served one tour in Iraq and earned the prestigious Iraqi Freedom Medal of Honor.

Dr. Monsano is the proud recipient of the President Lifetime Achievement Award and the Woman of Heart Award. An internationally recognized speaker, Dr. Monsano shares her expertise on the importance of having a positive mindset and empowering women to achieve their business goals.

Dr. Monsano is the CEO/Founder of Elite Creations, a branding and marketing agency that offers graphic design. Her vision expanded in

January 2023 with the creation of the Phenomenal Woman That's You Awards and Magazine. The awards have rapidly become a cornerstone event.

Dr. Nadia Monsano multifaceted career, from her honorable military service to her impactful entrepreneurial endeavors, reflects a life lived in service to others and a commitment to excellence. Her story is a powerful reminder of what determination, passion, and a desire to give back can achieve.

Bringing Up the Next Generation of Leaders

Katrina Tasby

Everywhere, society looks to the younger generation as the bearers of the future. Whether in politics, business, government, education, or community service, the next generation of leaders will play a major role in shaping the world we live in. However, the qualities required to lead with honesty, a moral compass, a vision for who they are, and responsibility do not always come naturally. Leadership sometimes must be nurtured, cultivated, and guided to prepare the younger generation to take on the world we are leaving behind and meet the challenges ahead. Leading the next generation is not simply about imparting knowledge, but about fostering resilience, emotional intelligence, and ethical decision-making.

I have an employee on "detail" (loaned) to my budget section at my federal government job. The good thing about her is that she is eager to learn everything necessary to potentially secure the job permanently. Three days into her detail, she asked me to extend it. I responded, "We need to get to the end of the detail first"; it ends in four months. Having someone like her makes imparting knowledge easier. They come half-ready, needing only some accommodations; everyone learns differently, so methods that worked for one employee might not work for her. Since her detail began, I can tell she is very open. She is the future of the organization!

On the other hand, the previous employee on detail had some budget experience and was a bit closed off. She was a very good worker, but stringent. Her emotional intelligence was lacking, creating difficulties between the staff and us. When I tried to guide her, I was met with "I know" or "yeah." She had an "I know it all" attitude. Although a team player willing to help, it came at a cost to the overall team.

What I Believe Future Leaders Need

Preparing the younger generation for leadership begins with exposing them to the diverse and complex challenges within their organizations. The foundation of good leadership lies in emotional intelligence—the ability to understand and manage one's emotions while recognizing and influencing the emotions of others. Empathy fosters connection and builds trust, allowing leaders to understand the perspectives of those who may not share their views, experiences, or backgrounds.

Leadership is not about having all the answers; it's about asking the right questions and knowing how to address complex issues. Cultivating critical thinking and problem-solving in young leaders is crucial. Challenges often arise with no quick fix. Leaders need the ability to navigate complicated problems and find innovative solutions. Integrity is integral to leadership. A leader must be trustworthy, and trust is built.

Finally, one of the most effective ways to develop the next generation of leaders is by providing opportunities to lead. Leadership cannot be fully understood as an idea alone; it must be practiced. Giving tomorrow's youth opportunities to take on leadership roles, even in small capacities, allows them to test their skills, learn from mistakes, and gain valuable insights into the challenges of leadership. The experience of leading builds self-confidence and a sense of responsibility—key qualities of effective leaders.

Conclusion

Developing the next generation of leaders is a significant undertaking that requires a commitment to developing the skills and moral character necessary for effective leadership. By focusing on emotional intelligence, critical thinking, problem-solving, and providing opportunities, we can ensure the younger generation is equipped to lead with integrity.

Katrina Tasby

Let me introduce - Katrina Tasby, but you might already know her as Trina The Realtor. Yes, that's right! She is your go-to expert for relocating to the vibrant, limitless city of Houston and its surrounding areas. But what you might not know is that she is so much more than a realtor. Why? Because her mission in life doesn't stop at closing real estate deals; it's about opening doors of opportunities, wisdom, and empowerment for you.

As a proud United States Air Force veteran and spouse, she gets it. Relocation isn't just about moving furniture from point A to point B. It's about transitioning your life, your dreams, and your aspirations.

When she first set foot in Houston back in November 2015, coming from the bustling avenues of Washington, DC, she knew that she was home.

And because she is something of a foodie, trust her when she says, "I've tasted the heart of this city", literally!

As a committed member of the Alpha Kappa Alpha Sorority her network and knowledge base are rock solid and ever-growing.

Let's talk about you for a second. Are you prepared to unlock your Growth Mindset? Because if you are, you going to get along just fine. Whether it's finding your dream home or upgrading your thought patterns, consider Katrina your personal guide.

The Leadership P.U.Z.Z.L.E.: Every Piece Counts

LuDrean Howard Peterson

"A team is like a puzzle; every jigsaw piece is important to solve a problem or complete a picture." ~ Mo Kuku

Mo Kuku's quote eloquently describes the synergy between leadership and teamwork, emphasizing how a leader's genuine understanding and appreciation of employees—viewing them as individuals beyond their tasks—fosters an environment where they feel valued and empowered. Each "jigsaw piece" signifies a team member whose unique skills and perspectives are vital in piecing together solutions or realizing collective visions. This analogy was profoundly illuminated during a significant team retreat, where it became evident that true leadership extends beyond task delegation—it involves seeing each individual as a critical component of the organizational tapestry.

Much like assembling a complex puzzle where each piece holds unique value, leaders who understand and appreciate their team members as individuals can inspire growth and learning. In today's dynamic work environment, leaders serve as powerful force multipliers, not by merely driving performance, but by empowering individuals to teach and influence others.

In this evolving landscape of leadership, recognizing that "every piece counts" is crucial to building resilient and cohesive teams. This chapter explores how acknowledging the essential nature of each team member transforms leaders into powerful force multipliers. Drawing from a pivotal team retreat experience, titled "Essential Piece," I highlight the importance of showing team members how their contributions connect to the organization's mission, emphasizing that each person is an essential piece in achieving overarching goals. Through open dialogue, I came to understand what was essential to them beyond their work tasks, recognizing them as whole individuals with unique perspectives and needs. This empathetic approach strengthened their connection to the mission and enhanced my leadership perspective, fostering a more inclusive and supportive environment.

From the enlightening retreat to practical applications of the P.U.Z.Z.L.E. framework, this narrative highlights how leaders can create environments where team members feel empowered to contribute their best by valuing every piece.

A Journey of Transformative Leadership

As I embarked on this phase of my leadership journey, I realized that one of the most empowering actions I could take was to facilitate environments where open dialogue was encouraged.

- **Retreat Realization:** During our team retreat, open dialogue revealed profound insights. Participants shared personal stories and expressed feelings of disconnection, shedding light on the crucial need for a leadership approach centered on empathy and personal connection. Each discussion unveiled the unique dynamics within the team, underscoring the importance of seeing team members not just as employees, but as whole individuals with distinct backgrounds, aspirations, and challenges.

- **Pivotal Moment:** The retreat's conclusion marked a pivotal moment in my leadership journey. The experience underscored the importance of valuing each team member holistically. This profound lesson has since become a cornerstone in shaping my leadership style, one that embraces empathy alongside efficiency.

- **Commitment to Cohesiveness:** This insight continues to influence my leadership policies and practices. The commitment to nurturing a holistic leadership approach empowered my team to excel by embracing their diverse contributions and nurturing their growth. By intertwining empathy with effectiveness, the leadership environment transformed into one where everyone thrived in unity and shared success.

This retreat was a pivotal moment in my leadership journey, emphasizing the importance of valuing each team member holistically. It taught me that when people feel genuinely cared for, they show remarkable support and dedication in return, creating a more cohesive and motivated team. This lesson has been a cornerstone in developing my leadership style, one that embraces empathy alongside efficiency.

P.U.Z.Z.L.E. Framework

Reflecting on the insightful dialogue and transparent communication at the retreat, I illustrated how each team member's role fits into the broader mission of our agency. This clarity renewed their sense of purpose and bolstered their confidence and engagement. However, the retreat was not just about imparting knowledge; it was a reciprocal experience. My team taught me to see each member as a holistic individual, emphasizing the need for empathy and deeper connection in enriching our leadership dynamics. The collective reflections and lessons learned led to the development of the P.U.Z.Z.L.E. framework.

This framework creates a ripple effect that enhances team dynamics and organizational outcomes. By appreciating the value of their contributions, team members connect more deeply with their work and the team's goals, driving us all toward shared success.

- **P - Participate with Purpose:** Engage authentically with your team. Active participation is the heartbeat of successful teams. As a leader, you can set the tone by not just directing, but engaging alongside your team members. Foster an environment where everyone feels their voice is vital to the collective goal.

- **U - Understand to Unite:** Cultivate an environment where open conversations are encouraged, allowing team members to express their unique communication styles, motivations, and preferences for recognition. By fostering a safe space for dialogue, leaders can gain a deeper understanding of individual aspirations and strengths. This understanding enables the alignment of tasks with personal capabilities, ensuring each member works at their highest potential.

- **Z - Zoning into a Shared Vision:** A pivotal part of leadership is cascading information effectively throughout all levels. During our retreat, I began with the agency's overarching mission, cascading this vision down through each center, office, division, team, and individual. This approach helped every team member see how their specific role contributes to the agency's overall success. By understanding the significance of their contributions, team members connected their daily tasks with the larger mission, fostering a sense of pride and purpose in their work.

- **Z - Zeroing in on Solutions:** Encourage a culture where team members feel empowered to approach you with solutions, not just problems. By openly sharing the types of questions I typically ask when faced with challenges, the team developed a proactive mindset. They started coming forward with problems already paired with potential solutions, which streamlined decision-making and enhanced their confidence and problem-solving skills.

- **L - Learn and Lead Together:** Foster a culture where learning and leading are intertwined, promoting growth at every level. Implement individual development plans as a fundamental tool, making them mandatory while providing freedom for individual engagement. Align these plans with stretch goals and strategic assignments that challenge team members to excel. Reward and compliment employees often. My team wanted to have more team gatherings. These gatherings further strengthened our team's bond, making learning and leading a shared, rewarding journey.

- **E - Engage Through Trust and Collaboration:** Lay a foundation of trust and collaboration by truly caring for team members as individuals, beyond their roles as workers. Create an inclusive and supportive work environment where everyone feels valued and respected. Facilitate open lines of communication and foster spaces for dialogue and brainstorming, motivating team members to share ideas freely, understanding that each piece is vital in completing the puzzle. By leveraging the power of trust and collaboration, innovation thrives, allowing the team to achieve excellence together.

This framework offers a roadmap for leaders to align personal and organizational goals, fostering an environment that encourages innovation and collaboration.

Conclusion

The essence of true leadership lies in illuminating the inherent value within each team member, transforming mere tasks into meaningful contributions to the greater mission. Leadership can be compared to a puzzle, where every piece has its place and significance. Through the insight shared from our transformative team retreat, I helped my team feel valued and understand that each of them was not just a team member, but an essential piece that collectively completed the office's puzzle. My journey with my team revealed that when individuals see themselves as vital pieces of the organizational puzzle, they unleash empowerment and engagement.

True leadership is a continuous journey of growth centered on cherishing each piece of the puzzle. Recognizing the indispensable nature of every individual transforms leaders into power enablers of success. By cherishing every piece, you strengthen your leadership capabilities and inspire those around you to strive for greatness.

In the ever-evolving landscape of leadership, understanding that "every piece counts" is crucial to building resilient and cohesive teams. This chapter explores how recognizing the essential nature of each team member transforms leaders into powerful force multipliers. Drawing from a pivotal team retreat experience, I realized the profound impact of viewing every team member as a unique and invaluable piece of the organizational puzzle. Valuing each team member as unique and indispensable transforms leaders into true catalysts of success and growth. The retreat has also shown that effective leadership is about not just guiding tasks, but fostering genuine connections and empowering individuals to contribute meaningfully to a larger purpose.

The P.U.Z.Z.L.E. framework serves as a guiding light for leaders seeking to create environments where everyone feels integral and valued. By embracing these principles, leaders can transform their teams into cohesive, dynamic units capable of extraordinary achievements. Leaders can drive their teams towards unparalleled achievements by choosing to:

- **P** - Participate with Purpose
- **U** - Understand to Unite
- **Z** - Zone into a Shared Vision
- **Z** - Zero in on Solutions
- **L** - Learn and Lead Together, Continuously
- **E** - Engage Through Trust and Collaboration

As you move forward, let these insights enlighten your leadership journey. By nurturing each piece, you create an environment where unity and collaboration are the foundations of unparalleled success. In embracing this philosophy and acting as a catalyst for both individual and collective greatness, you prove that each piece is essential. Every voice, every contribution, every individual piece matters! Celebrating this diversity and synergy crafts a lasting legacy of inclusive and effective leadership—a journey where every piece indeed counts!

LuDrean Howard Peterson

LuDrean Howard Peterson is an inspirational leader renowned for transforming visions into successful outcomes. With over 33 years in Human Resources, she has served in senior leadership roles at the FDA and is an established results-driven project manager, leading initiatives in the U.S. and internationally, including China, India, South Africa, Latin America, Europe, and Mexico.

As CEO of Delivering on Ideas & Thoughts (DOIT), she specializes in turning DREAMERS into DOERS, empowering individuals and organizations to achieve their dreams. She also founded Do It Empowers, Inc., a philanthropic nonprofit focused on uplifting underserved communities by promoting empowerment and addressing grief and socioeconomic challenges.

Additionally, LuDrean is an international host and emcee, known for engaging audiences with her insightful commentary. She hosts the "Let's Do It" Talk Show and is an acclaimed author of best-selling books on grief and healing, also co-authoring nine other projects.

Academically, she holds dual master's degrees in Business Administration and Management, alongside a Master Certification in Project Management. As an Adjunct Trainer at Lakeside Global Institute, she focuses on trauma and grief.

Personally, LuDrean is a devoted mother and grandmother who enjoys traveling, shopping, reading, and meaningful conversations.

Connect with LuDrean:

Website: http://www.do-it-delivers.com

Facebook: LuDrean Peterson

Instagram: @do_it_delivers

Reflection Page: Becoming a Force Multiplier in Leadership

Now you've read through the book in its entirety and how can you leverage the lessons, strategies, and tips to become a force multiplier to elevate others to new heights.

A "force multiplier" is a person or thing that, when applied, significantly increases the impact or effectiveness of a particular effort. As a leader, your ability to be a force multiplier for your team, organization, or community can exponentially enhance success, innovation, and growth. Use the following questions to reflect on how you can become a more effective force multiplier.

1. Understanding Your Leadership Impact

- How do you currently measure your impact as a leader?
  _____
  _____
  _____
  _____
  _____

- In what ways can you amplify the efforts of those around you, rather than simply focusing on your own contributions?
  _____
  _____
  _____
  _____
  _____

- Are there areas where you might be unintentionally limiting your team's potential? If so, how can you address these barriers?
  _____
  _____
  _____
  _____

2. Empowering Others

- How do you empower your team members to take ownership of their work and ideas?

- How often do you delegate responsibilities, and do you allow others the space to lead in areas where they have expertise?

- What specific actions can you take to cultivate a growth mindset within your team?

3. Building Trust and Collaboration

- How do you create an environment where your team feels safe to take risks and fail without fear of judgment?

- How do you ensure that your leadership fosters collaboration and mutual respect among team members?

- Reflect on a time when you successfully collaborated with others to achieve a goal. What did you learn from that experience that could help you in the future?

4. Enhancing Communication

- Are you actively listening to the needs, concerns, and ideas of your team? How can you improve your communication to ensure you're fully understanding them?

- How can you ensure that your communication is clear, transparent, and aligns with your team's goals and values?

- How do you adapt your communication style to different individuals or teams to increase effectiveness?

5. Developing Future Leaders

- How are you mentoring or coaching others to step into leadership roles?

- What steps are you taking to identify and nurture potential leaders within your organization?

- Are you actively creating opportunities for others to gain the skills and experience they need to lead?

6. Fostering Innovation and Creativity

- How do you encourage your team to think outside the box and challenge the status quo?

  _____
  _____
  _____
  _____
  _____
  _____

- In what ways can you create a culture that values experimentation, even when results are uncertain?

  _____
  _____
  _____
  _____
  _____
  _____

- How do you reward and recognize innovative thinking within your team?

  _____
  _____
  _____
  _____
  _____
  _____

7. Creating Systems and Structures

- What systems or processes can you implement to help your team be more efficient and effective?

  _____
  _____
  _____
  _____
  _____
  _____

- How do you ensure that resources—time, money, and energy—are being used in the most impactful ways?

  _____
  _____
  _____
  _____
  _____
  _____

- Are you actively removing bottlenecks or obstacles that could hinder your team's performance?

  _____
  _____
  _____
  _____
  _____
  _____

8. Self-Reflection and Growth

- How do you evaluate your own strengths and weaknesses as a leader?

  _____
  _____
  _____
  _____
  _____
  _____

- What specific habits or behaviors do you need to develop to become a more effective force multiplier?

  _____
  _____
  _____
  _____
  _____
  _____

- How can you stay committed to your own personal development, and how will that benefit your team?

9. Sustaining Momentum

- How do you maintain motivation and drive when faced with challenges or setbacks?

- What strategies can you employ to keep your team energized and focused over the long term?

- How do you celebrate both small and large wins to maintain a culture of success?

10. Impact Beyond the Team

- How can your leadership efforts create ripple effects beyond your immediate team or organization?

- Are you actively engaging with other leaders and stakeholders to share knowledge and multiply the impact of your initiatives?

- How can you contribute to broader community or industry growth by fostering collaboration and growth at scale?

Action Steps:

1. Commit to One Change: Based on your reflections, identify one specific action you can take to become a more effective force multiplier.

2. Seek Feedback: Ask for feedback from colleagues, team members, or mentors about how they perceive your leadership style and effectiveness in multiplying impact.

_____
_____
_____
_____
_____

3. Set Milestones: Create a plan to implement and track your progress in the next 30, 60, and 90 days. What short-term steps will help you build momentum toward becoming a better leader?

_____
_____
_____
_____
_____

Use these questions regularly to assess and refine your leadership approach, making sure your actions multiply the potential of those around you!

For Further Reflection

Made in the USA
Columbia, SC
13 February 2025